Sergei Shargunov

A BOOK WITHOUT PHOTOGRAPHS

The Secret Album

Glagoslav Publications

A Book Without Photographs
The Secret Album
by Sergei Shargunov

Translated from the Russian by Simon Patterson
Edited by Scott D. Moss and Camilla Stein

© 2012, Alpina Non-Fiction

© 2013, Glagoslav Publications, United Kingdom

Glagoslav Publications Ltd
88-90 Hatton Garden
EC1N 8PN London
United Kingdom

www.glagoslav.com

ISBN: 978-1-78267-051-3

This book is in copyright. No part of this publication may be reproduced, stored in a retrieval system or transmitted in any form or by any means without the prior permission in writing of the publisher, nor be otherwise circulated in any form of binding or cover other than that in which it is published without a similar condition, including this condition, being imposed on the subsequent purchaser.

Contents

My Soviet Childhood 6
How I Was An Altar Boy 5
Schools 25
About You, Girls 44
Grandma And The Journalism Faculty. 54
The Bolbases 65
Protest On The Run 77
The Adventures Of The Rabble 83
Afterwards 98
To Chechnya, To Chechnya! 111
In The War 130
How I Fired My Friend 139
Revolution In Asia. 155
Voskresenki. 170

Photographs never leave you. They stay with you all your life, and after you are dead.

A cemetery is a photo album. Many faces, usually festive and welcoming. Virtually at the moment when the flash was fired, people thought about where their photos would go. And those smiles? The surname, the years of life and a calm face that believes in immortality. All around, the buzzing of flies, plants, other faces, who also don't know that they are masks behind which decay runs rampant.

Once, as I walked through a wide Moscow cemetery, I met my next-door neighbor. Feeling someone's gaze on me, I turned my head to the left and found myself looking right into the face of Ivan Frolovich Sokov from apartment 110. He was dressed up for an occasion, in a general's uniform. The photograph was mounted on black, polished marble: the sun was reflecting in it, blinding me. "So we've met once more," I thought. "An accidental meeting, like in a crowd, somewhere in the metro…."

But we are also photographed before we are born.

I remember: Anya came back from the doctor with a large plastic sheet with a strange display of light and shade frozen on it.

"That's a he," she exclaimed.

It was our son, an unborn fetus, the future Vanechka.

My life began when photography was highly valued. Solitary amateur wizards in dark rooms developed film, which drew envy and awe from children. For the first seven years of my life I am only photographed in black and white. Then came color photos, although they were on paper. After twenty-five, almost everything is digital, in an enormous quantity.

I believe in the secret of photography, which has yet to be revealed.

A BOOK WITHOUT PHOTOGRAPHS

Photos taken from space allow us to see the inner layers of the earth. A person's ailments can be determined from a photograph. We are bewitched by photographs: they enchant us and put curses on us. It may not often be successful, but there is a nasty game popular among the people: to spoil the photo of an enemy. Now this enchantment is probably made easier due to the possibilities of Photoshop.

One woman selling goods at the village shop said quite ingenuously:

"I have a whole pile of photos of me. On Saturday night I sit by the oven, I stroke them, stroke and stroke, and throw them in the fire. To make myself young! To make my wrinkles go away…." She laughed flirtatiously.

There's a whole avalanche of photographs these days, and video clips, the world is full of them, the world is crazy about recording things. But at the same time, it's considered old-fashioned to get worried about photographs. They're obtained too easily and lose their value. Perhaps photographs were left behind in the 20th century, and are increasingly turning into garbage….

I have few photographs. I don't collect them and don't keep them. But that's not important. I constantly return to events and people who have been photographically imprinted in my brain. And this book will probably be continued.

Sometimes I think that all of my photographs, lost, missing or never taken, are kept somewhere. Some day they will be developed.

Perhaps, when there is no longer any choice (in the next war or on my death bed), I will see this album of my life, which was leafed through hurriedly and mercilessly.

And then I will understand some vital secret, I will gasp in amazement and, relieved, sink blindly into death.

My Soviet Childhood

It was the autumn of 1993. I ran out of the house to the barricades.

Here there were poor people, and others not so poor, and the only slogan that everyone took up readily was: "The Soviet Union!"

I stood on the square by a large white building, which seemed to have been made of steam and smoke, and all around – in drizzle and smoke – the departing Russia shuffled from side to side. The love and pain of the trusting faces, the wild flailing of arms, the smudged posters. The hot light of defeat came from the red flags.

"The Sooooviet Union!" The cry came rolling, wave after wave.

"The Sooooviet Union!" The entire square sings, moans and groans in desperation and fury.

Next to me there is an old woman. Decrepit and shivering, she doesn't chant, but she utters the name of her Motherland in a protracted whine....

From a distant balcony we are promised that soon military units, faithful to their oath, will come here – into the fog and smoke....

In my childhood, I didn't like the Soviet Union, I couldn't like it, that was how I was brought up.

But at the age of 30, when the Union had already perished, following a whim, I ran to the square of the outcasts, who were shouting with all their might, summoning its spirit....

...I had learned to read before I learned to write. I took musty books with cloth covers, without titles, in home-made, crude bindings. I opened them, saw the mysterious blurry black and white pictures, and copied the letters. Sometimes the letters bent like a candle flame:

it was a bad Xerox. The books attracted me because they were forbidden. The lives of the saints murdered by the Bolsheviks, collected in America by the Nun Taisiya. In this way, I gradually learned to read.

I was four years old, and Mama called us to supper. Papa and our guest, the ginger-bearded Sasha, were walking to the kitchen along the narrow corridor, and I followed them.

"I'll have to collect the books..." the guest mumbled, and suddenly they stopped as if riveted to the spot, because my father grabbed him hard by the elbow.

"Books?" he asked in a stony voice. "What books?"

For a second they exchanged glances. Sasha tore himself away from the floor and, in a light jump, he touched the low ceiling of the corridor with his fingers. And he said:

"A children's book," with joy and terror.

Then, in a strange, noiseless dance, they approached the kitchen, both stretching out their right arms with their index fingers, excitedly towards the corner of the window sill where the telephone lay in green modesty.

In the kitchen doorway I started running, pushed forward, risking being trampled on, and I remembered those fingers that pierced the warm, satiated air.

I remember the scene as if I had observed it a minute ago. Everything unfolded swiftly, but so vividly that for a moment I felt the excitement of the carnival.

Rushing to the telephone, I grabbed the receiver, and feverishly shouted:

"Books! Books! Books!"

Mama dropped the frying pan, Papa pulled the plug out of the socket and gave me a burning slap, and the guest grabbed me, crying, by the elbow with a predatory movement, trained his bright dry eyes on me and murmured with a whistle out of his ginger beard:

"Do you want your Papa to go to jail? You won't have a Papa...."

Some years later I found out that my father, who was a priest, was the owner of a small underground printing press hidden in a hut somewhere near Ryazan. There several initiates, including the guest, printed books: prayer books and the lives of saints (mainly new martyrs, including the last imperial family) from templates sent from the town of Jordanville, New York. And these missionary books were then sent all over Russia. If news of this had been leaked, I would have become the son of a prisoner. The telephone is the main weapon for listening in, members of the underground believe. It is alive. It even listens when the receiver is hung up. "Books, books" were the key words and the prickly words that were not supposed to be said.

I was five years old when the husband of Irina, a friend of our family, was arrested in Kiev. She visited us with her daughter Ksenia. A grey, scared, cowed girl with large serious eyes. Her father was put in jail for a book. He was hammering away on the typewriter, and supposedly people had come to search the apartment after they had heard this noise of the keys through the telephone.

At the age of six I also started working on a book. Not because I wanted to go to jail, I was simply lured by the forbidden aspect. I drew various priests, monarchs and archbishops who had suffered during the period of Soviet power. This book, with clumsy childish scrawls and bearded faces in monks' caps, was taken away from me by my parents. I didn't want to give them the large exercise book, and hid it in my pillowcase, but they found it and took it away. The smell of burning paper came wafting from the kitchen. They were afraid.

But I continued to draw and write protest pamphlets and banned lives of saints. And once, pretending to be scared, I decided to destroy the heap of what I had just drawn and written – this was a rehearsal in case there was suddenly a search of the apartment. I decided not to burn the pages, but to flush them down the drain. I gathered them up and put them in a toy bath, and for some reason I also put a photograph of myself there from a time which I didn't remember: as a blissful infant, I was dipped in a baptismal font by the blissful and grey-haired Father Nikolai Sitnikov. For some reason, I thought that this photo was also a piece of incriminating evidence. I put the papers and photo together and poured water over them; the ink ran, and soon the forbidden objects turned into colored paper porridge. My parents noticed that the photograph had gone missing, but I didn't admit to them what had happened to it.

And then, like in Rybakov's thrilling *The Cutlass* (I played the role of the bad boy, the son of a counterrevolutionary priest), the remains of the last imperial family came to our apartment. A writer had dug up the remains in a Ural swamp and gave part of them to the priest.

Buttons, fabric, a broach, a skull and bones – this was all taken in by the child's eyes, but the child's lips had a lock on them. The world did not yet know about this find. The USSR did not know. Nor did Moscow. Or Frunzenskaya embankment. Or the courtyard. The neighbor Vanka didn't know.

So that's how I spent my Soviet childhood – in the same apartment as the imperial family.

(A paradox: my grandmother Valeria, my mother's mother, studied in Yekaterinburg in the same class as the daughter of Yurovsky, who shot the Tsar).

A year after the remains appeared in our apartment, Zhanna came to visit (and I remember now that it was raining heavily), a French diplomat with a simple peasant's face. She was a Catholic, and adored the Orthodox Church. Foreigners were not allowed to leave Moscow, but she would tie a scarf around her head, catch the train to Zagorsk in the morning, stand for the entire liturgy at the Trinity Monastery and come back to Moscow. Perhaps the Chekists were indulgent towards this devout foreigner.

She gave me a packet of sweets, refused to have tea, and went straight to my father in his study. And they began to do something there. I thought I could hear the chirping of a mad grasshopper. Unable to withstand it, I opened the door and went in on tiptoes. Zhanna kept changing her pose. She hovered around the table. One of her eyes was shut, and by her other eye she held a large black camera, which emitted bluish flashes with a chirping sound. The table was covered with a red Easter tablecloth, and on top of it bones and skulls lay at equal distance, items I was already familiar with.

I drew closer. For some reason, my father was wearing a black cassock and standing by the iconostasis, over the open drawer, where a pile of copper buttons, a large broach with stones, two silver bracelets and green strips of material were awaiting their turn to be placed on the table.

When he saw me, he waved his hand noiselessly, sending me away. The sleeve of his cassock billowed like a wing.

During that time, my uncle was making a career for himself in the system. Uncle came to visit us once every half year from Sverdlovsk, where he worked at the regional committee.

My uncle was a model Soviet man. Gagarin style. A handsome man. Muscular, lively, cheerful, with a face always ready to break into a smile. A courageous and broad smile. He had a black tuft on his head, dimples on his cheeks, and a champagne sparkle in his eyes. He had a fine, optimistic voice. Uncle Gena remembered the entire Soviet pop repertoire off by heart, and could sing it well. When he visited, he spread a smell of eau de cologne, he and my father drank a few shots, my uncle wrapped himself in a red pile dressing gown, got up before daylight, did gymnastics for half an hour, shaved and snorted under the water and went away wearing a suit, collected and elegant, out on official business all day.

But once he visited without any smiles. He threw his coat on to the sofa in the corridor. He didn't put on slippers, and walked around in socks. He sat on the side of the couch, hunched over. He didn't even bring me a treat, although once he had given me a heavy pinecone with delicious nuts.

"Brother, you've killed me…." My uncle's voice trembled, and became terrifyingly tender. "You've ruined my career. I couldn't talk about it over the phone. Now Struchkov has won. Everything was going swimmingly for me. Yeltsin summoned me. He said: "Is your brother a priest? How is that? How?" And he trampled me.

Uncle took a shot glass, turned it around, looked inside, and nervously asked, as if this were the most important thing:

"Why aren't you pouring me anything?"

"Who's Yeltsin?" Papa asked.

"My boss, did you forget?" Uncle loudly inhaled, opened the bottle and filled the glass. "Don't you care about my life? Do you know how many people he's eaten alive? We had Voropaev. He tormented Ptukhin to the point of a heart attack. Yeltsin is a rock! You'll hear more about him! He won't look…. You give him an inch…. He slaughtered Pyotr Nikanorovich Kozlov on his birthday. He congratulated him by firing him, how do you like that?" Without finishing, uncle, with the resolution of a suicide, poured the contents of the glass fully into his mouth, jumped up and walked around the kitchen.

Mama said, reasonably:

"Gennady, sit down, why are you so worried. Don't you think this isn't so serious against the background of life: Kozlov, Ptukhin, who else did you name? Suchkov, right? Yelkin…."

"Not Yelkin, Yeltsin! Not Suchkov, Struchkov!" Uncle stamped his foot on the linoleum. "It's the state apparatus! It's power! It's your fate and mine, everyone's! Why did you become a priest? Not for yourself, not for others…. You'll dry up, and there won't be any life for your family!"

Then I sat in the other room and heard the noise of the quarrel coming from the kitchen. So from a very early age I knew that there were few people one could talk to openly.

There was a priest whom my parents suspected of being a KGB agent. And they said: "Forgive us, Lord, if we are wrong to sin against an innocent man!" He visited Papa with persistent regularity, and when he visited, I was told: "shh!" His name was Father Terenty. He gave off an aroma of incense. I took blessing from him, breathed the fragrant warmth of his soft hands, but didn't talk to him anymore than I had to. He had long black and grey hair and a fox-like expression on his face. He constantly lowered his eyelids meekly. He had a chronic cold. He wiped his nose with a handkerchief. This cold caused him to have a worn-down, wet voice.

"Father Terenty," mother said to him, seeing him off, "why do you visit us when you're ill? We have a small child."

And in these words, there was a hint at something else – do you visit us with a clear conscience, dear Father Terenty?

I heard the adults' discussions about foreign countries. But in my dreams, I had never been aboard, I was happy to muck about here. I valued our apartment in an enormous building with a spire and the wooden house at the dacha. I wanted to dig ditches, crawl in the trenches, hide with a weapon behind the fir tree, biting the branch and feeling the bitter and stick evergreen juice on my teeth. Clay and the dust from the roads – this was the "calling card" of the war I craved. I liked dirt and dust…. Yes, I jumped for hours on the sofa, raising up columns of dust, as if I were driving in a cart surrounded by divisions, and we were travelling across the country. There were shots, armor, cracking sounds, white flashes on the night-time horizon, injured friends, but not mortally, and a dark blond girl of my age pressed her head against the commander's chest. We were six years old. A children's crusade. And our

A BOOK WITHOUT PHOTOGRAPHS

hearts worked precisely, like motors: tick-tick-tick. And the white flash connected us.

The capture of Moscow. Wind and victory. Windswept days. We would rebuild the Church of Christ the Savior from the blueprints. We would equip an expedition for the rescued altar that was taken abroad, and take down the preserved bas-relief of the Donskoy Cathedral. My Papa would say a prayer on the Moscow River, and sprinkle the heavy, salty drops of city water into the holy water vial, and the building of the enormous church would begin. And at the same time, special services would purify this dirty river, so that it was resurrected, cheered up, and you could swim in it again, like in the olden days.

This was my dream.

Now I imagine different things.

I would be a Soviet writer. No, listen to me: imagine, I'm a Soviet writer. And what then?

What about the others? A collective farmer? A worker? A scientist? A soldier? A teacher? A doctor? I think that everyone travels in time and imagines oneself there.

I was hostile to the Soviet Union all my childhood, and I did not join the Octobrists – the first child in the entire history of the school. I didn't join the pioneers either.

But I still miss the Homeland of my childhood. I remember the feeling of genuineness: winter was winter, autumn was autumn, and summer was summer. I remember the atmosphere of a big village all around, where a scandal between strangers was always homely, the singing women's voices, the hoarse men's voices, and the voices sound so carefree and pacified, that this couldn't even be hidden from a child.

In the autumn of '93, although it was already late, I returned my debt to the Soviet Union as a teenager. I ran away from home, and rushed to the square.

The people gathered there were raw, the steam mixed with smoke. Through the grey haze, fires occasionally sparkled, as if the sun were pitifully trying to escape from the mire.

The next day, a newspaper photograph of the square was printed – the last rally before the white building was surrounded in barbed wire. The photograph was taken from the balcony. It was a good photo, even though it was black and white. Faces thrown back, fists clenched, flags raised…. The people shouted: "The Soviet Union!"

Where I was standing, the abundant smoke was billowing, covering fifty or so heads, and so I am not visible in the photograph.

How I Was An Altar Boy

I not only encountered the anti-Soviet underground. I also encountered the Red Church – an important part of the Soviet Union.

At the age of four, during Easter Week, I found myself at the altar for the first time. In the church of the Consolation of All Sorrows, which resembled a stone cake, large and resonant, with a round dome and dramatic marble angles on the walls inside.

Years later I recreate this picture for myself.

Archbishop Kiprian was a true actor (by profession and calling). A grey, short, stout wizard. He liked the theater, restaurants and the bathhouse. Kiprian was Soviet and worldly, although they said he was passionately devout. He was a charming sort of pushy holiday-maker. He went up to the pulpit and denounced the neutron bomb, which kills people but leaves things behind. This was a symbol of the West. (He even went to agitate for the "Reds" when he visited the Priest Men and Professor Shafarevich). On New Year, he called for people not to observe the Christmas fast: "Drink sweetly, eat sausage!" He also said about communion in heaven: "We have somewhere for a person to go. The communal council! The communal committee! The communal social serpentry (security that is) department!" He wasn't really worried about mentioning the serpent in the latter. He told Papa about Voroshilov singing at a banquet in the Kremlin. He came up and sang the complex troparian for moving the relics of the enlightener Nikolay, in a bass voice. My mother remembered Kiprian when he was young and had jet black hair. When she was a girl, she lived nearby and came to the church. "On your knees! Stalin is ill," and people collapsed on to the stone slabs of this large church. Stone slabs covered in places by iron ornaments.

Once Kiprian took us home in his Volga.

"Does your husband let you go to the theater? Or to the cinema?" He asked Mama.

He asked me in the car:

"Is your Papa strict?"

"He's kind," I squeaked, to the delight of my parents.

"Does he let you watch TV?"

"Yes," I lied. We did not have a TV set.

And so, at the age of four, in the year when Andropov was replaced by Chernenko, on Easter week I went on to the altar for the first time.

There were no surplices, or gowns, for such a young altar boy, and I stayed in my shirt and pants with suspenders. The archbishop hugged my head, bending over with a sigh: the foam of his beard, red lips, a lavish golden hat with enamel icons sewn into it. He kissed my cheeks: "Christ has risen! What should you reply? You haven't forgotten? You're a hero!" He put me on an iron chair, and put an old iron-bound New Testament on my knees. It was the size of my body.

Then he stood next to me, bent over and hugged my neck (the sleeve of his robe was tenderly smooth), and hissed:

"Look, my dear, now the fish will come out!"

An old nun in black, with a large steel camera, made a barely audible click.

I remembered forever that Kiprian said fish instead of bird. Perhaps because we were at the altar, and the fish is an ancient symbol of the Church.

Unlike Papa, who was concentrated, serious and rejected the Soviet regime, the others at the altar looked relaxed. There was the deacon Gennady, a loud and jolly man, with ruddy cheeks and little round glasses. He deliberately did not wear a beard ("Angels don't have beards"). "And it was raised to the sky on a wire", he read out to the entire church, confusing some Church

Slavonic word, and then laughed at his mistake, shaking his cheeks and patting his stomach under the satin fabric, and asked himself: "In an elevator or something?"

In the years of freedom that followed, he would be beaten up in a train and be punched in the eye along with the lens of his glasses….

At the altar, the old lady in a black gown, Maria, was there, who told me off kindly and drank kagor wine with boiling water out of a silver cup – the drink was the same color as the cover of the book by Mayakovsky, *My Years Are Growing*, which she gave me as a present on the 1st of May.

"Mother Maria, where is my photograph?" I asked.

"What photograph?"

"That one! With his Grace! When I came to you the first time!"

"Quiet, don't be so noisy, you shout louder than the choir…"

There is a card at home. In a safe place. I am making an important album. The priest blessed it. I include everyone who serves with us: both old and young….

Towards the end of her life she will lose her apartment to conmen….

I think with horror: what if no monastery took her in? Where did she live out her days? And what happened to the album? Was it thrown out in the trash?

Also at the altar was Archpriest Boris, the future superior. He liked borshch and pies with innards (his mother cooked them very well). The meaty face of a pirate with a crooked scar covered over with rough bristles. He shouted at the altar boys: "Seven nannies have a child without an eye!" He imitated the archbishop in his theatricality. He prayed, mumbling and sniffling, turning his eyes to the seven-branched candlestick: his hands upraised and his palms outstretched. The crimson curtain rustled behind him. I watched him with bated breath.

In 1991, Father Boris will support the emergency committee, and when the tanks leave Moscow, he will suddenly become old, sleepy and indifferent to everything....

Behind the threshold of the altar there was another steward, a secular person appointed by the authorities ("a KGB man", my parents whispered), a handsome Scottish earl with a bare skull, silent and sad, but every time he gave me a sweet and winked playfully.

And the priest Kiprian died here, in this beautiful spacious church, in the attic, where the long stone steps led, on a March morning, not long before Perestroika. His heart stopped. There was a legend among the old women that he tripped on the steps and rolled down them, but that wasn't true, of course.

During Perestroika, churches were permitted to ring bells. The bells hadn't been hung up yet. The chorister of the left choir, a red-haired, pointy-nosed lady, dragged me with her – under the dome, to investigate. For some reason the path was terribly difficult. For half an hour we clambered up rusty steps, sneezed among the yellow piles of Stalin-era newspapers, choked in narrow and endless passages, but finally reached the bare platform, which was white and slippery from bird droppings. I stood on the final step, sticking my head out of the manhole. The woman, bravely climbing out, tottered on one leg and almost fell down, but I grabbed her other leg, and her grey skirt covered my head like a tent.

I loved this solemn, enormous church, I was almost never bored there, although I was my father's prisoner. I continued the service at home, but played at being a priest. I read out prayers, waved watches on a chain, like a censer and shook Mama's headscarf over a can with needles in it, like a wimple over a chalice....

It was in the evening, when I was playing at being a priest who was at work, I looked into the bathroom, where the mechanic was making a racket.

"Playing at being a priest!" He spoke tiredly and irritably, making me freeze. "Don't pretend you weren't. I've got ears in my head. Remember my words: don't believe in it! I used to go to church too, my mother was terribly devout. Then I listened to a broadcast, I looked at the people there, old and stupid, and the ones who take their money, and goodbye. Thanks, I've had enough of that!" he passed his hand across his throat.

Neither dead nor alive, I went out of the bathroom, and sat silently in my room, listening for him to leave.

At the age of nine I was finally dressed in a surplice sewed specially by the nun Maria, white, with gold threads, with gilded round buttons on the side, and so long that my shoes could not be seen.

I began to go out to the people with a big candle during the reading of the Gospel. I remember standing there the first time, and the candle was heavy and swayed, the wax poured over my hands, it felt like a cat was scratching me, but I had to endure it. But afterwards it was pleasant to peel off the hardened cold shell. At the age of nine, I also read out a prayer to the whole church for the first time – for Communion. Choking, drowning, diving, my voice rang out in my ears – whining and unpleasant, and one thought turned in my head among the Slavonic words: what if I get stuck and stop speaking, what if I stop, if I shut the prayer book now, and run away into the noise of the cars – what then?

Before the collapse of the USSR, Papa was given a white church nearby us, I was eleven at the time. Inside there were sewing workshops, machines on two stories, the workers did not want to leave and argued with the community that was throwing them out – quite correctly sensing that reality was no longer required. I remember the first prayer at the church. The crowd prayed among the ruins, and the candles flickered among the bricks. A small part of the church was fenced off with plywood, and despite the chimes of the censer a telephone rang, and despite the choir an angry woman's voice was heard: "Hello! Speak up, Olya! They're making a racket!" – and despite the incense, tobacco smoke came wafting in, but the days of the office with a long, difficult name were over.

The church was restored quickly. Behind the Soviet layer, as if from a spell, the pre-Soviet layer was revealed. A fresco appeared on the vault: the miracle on Tiveriadsky Lake, realism from the late 19th century: a lot of blue, muscular bodies, an underwater pod of fish, and a boat. In the courtyard, where the pipes were being replaced, a cemetery was found, and a cardboard box full of dark bones, which had been preserved from the elements under a truck behind the church, and after a service they were buried, I lit the coals for the censer and burnt my finger so badly that my fingernail turned black and fell off. In the church itself, an elusive cricket appeared – a hooligan who liked to reply to the priest's intoning quicker than the choir did. The path to the bell tower proved to be quite easy – it was straight. It took all day to raise the bells up. On the next morning, before daylight, I clanged the metal against metal and got quite carried away, making a din. A fellow from a nearby apartment woke up in terror in a new world and barged into the church, begging to be allowed to sleep.

The son of the superior, I began to be an altar boy, already guessing that everyone around me – boys and men – were doomed by the laws of this flowing life, by the laws of any human society, to disappear sooner or later. The boys would grow up and tell their devout mothers to get lost, some would get offended by something and tear off their surplices, some would put on a monk's tonsure or become priests and go to another parish. Some would die, like one fine man, blue-eyed, black-bearded, with a thin voice, who loved the Virgin Mother. He stayed off drugs for years, but a girlfriend from his past came to visit, and he snapped and died soon afterwards….

By the age of twelve I started to find it boring in the

church, but I was an obedient son. I still dreamed of adventures: a fire, or crazed Satanists would attack the church – I'd be a hero and save everything, and Tonya, a girl from a large family, would blush with admiration. Small, gentle and silken, she would stand there with her bespectacled Mama and eight natural and adopted brothers and sisters at the front of the congregation: I would look at her through the crack in the altar door and roll a ball of wax between my fingers.

In the autumn of 1992, when I came with my father to the evening service, early as always, I had an adventure.

There were not many people, just a dozen, my father went behind the altar, and I was delayed and suddenly turned around at a sudden noise. From a distant corner of the church a person came running, clutching a rectangular item to his chest. An icon! He tore the iron door open. "Lord!" a woman sighed from near the candle holder, who was deaf as a post.

I didn't feel the cold in my shirtless vest, worn over my blue coat. He was running down Bolshaya Ordynka Street. Children run easily, and I almost caught up with him. He looked over his shoulder and began to walk at a broad pace. I also stopped for a second, but then ran even faster, although I could see myself from the outside: small and vulnerable.

He stood by the white stone gates of The Martha and Mary Convent. His hands on his chest. I stooped five paces away with clenched fists and a thumping heart.

He said quietly:

"Right, little brat! Get lost!"

"Give me the icon!" I shouted.

He quickly turned his head, looking around the street. No one had come to help me. There were hardly any passersby on this autumn evening. He had a beard that stuck out like an axe. Perhaps he had let it grow specially, so he didn't draw suspicion in churches.

"What icon?" He said even more quietly.

"Our icon!" I made a step forward and added with doubt: "It's under your jacket."

"Good night, kid!" he said distinctly.

He turned around abruptly, and with unexpected ability he raced off, ran across the road again and disappeared.

I ran after him – and walked back. The bell was ringing. At the entrance to the church there were lots of people, they milled about, welcoming me with smiles, not knowing what had happened. I nodded to them and for some reason did not go in immediately, as if I would be recognized as the thief.

I once saw what happened to icons in the church. The Sanctifier Nikolai was covered with moisture, and father was reading the service. I stood to the side of the icon, and held the book before my father, and after he read the turn-over point I turned the page. And I looked at the mysterious, yellow-brown icon, thick as a bar of bronze, along which newborn shining stripes moved. Then I kissed it after the other ones, breathing in the thickly sweet gentle smell. As I kissed it, I thought: "Why, why do I feel indifferent?"

At that service, we were photographed by the icon, but it was more that the icon was photographed, and one photograph also shed tears.

I was taken to the most varied holy places, monasteries, I was shown incorruptible relics and weeping images, I met famous elders and preachers, and I dove headfirst into icy-cold springs, but remained uninvolved.

I went everywhere, with the exception of the Church of the Grave of the Lord in Jerusalem at Easter, where it was believed the heavenly fire sinks and holy prayers are mixed with the flashes of cameras….

Were there epiphanies, did I feel the grace of God?

There was something else. On a humid summer's day, I read the entire liturgy, and at the prayer, at the last sounds things begin to turn black before my eyes. In complete darkness together with everyone else I approached the altar stand with the icon of the holiday, laid my forehead against it with a crack, and, intuitively recognizing the kind bell-ringing woman, whispered "I'm dying..." – and fell on top of her.

Or, in the morning, in the frost, I was breaking up ice by the porch, and the red sun was burning my sleepy eyes, in the warmth of the altar I knelt, spread out my arms, lowered my head, and through the acrid smoke of the incense I did not notice myself falling asleep.

There was something else as well: the farewell religious procession. At the age of seventeen, at Easter, I walked in front of the procession with a wooden stick on which was a lantern with four panes of colored glass, inside of which there was a flame flickering on a wick. It was before the end of school. I hadn't been going to church for a long time, but on this night I dressed in a bright yellow confectionary surplice and walked – for the sake of the holiday and to please Papa.

I held the lantern evenly and firmly, like a professional, and quietly sang along with the prayer song that I had known since childhood. The priests followed in heavy red robes, carrying red candles. Cameras flashed. The warm wind brought the singing of the girls' choir and the drone of many people, who (I say this without seeing) shuffled clumsily, because they constantly lit each other's candles, and during the procession each one would lose the flame and go back, several times. But my flame was protected by glass. I walked slowly, confidently, singing, my thoughts were far away....

Youth lay before me, which was so unlike childhood. I squinted my eyes at a bright spot. The billboard beyond the fence: "The night is yours! Add fire!" "I'll give a few triple kisses, then go out and smoke," I thought with the dull self-satisfaction of a teenager and sang a little louder: "Angels sing in the heavens...," and unexpectedly felt a twinge inside me.

I always remembered that spring night five minutes before Easter, I yelled "Truly he has risen!" and sang loudly, my cheeks burned, and I exchanged a triple kiss with everyone.

And I did not go out for the entire service, as if I was drawn to the naked wire.

But then came my youth anyway, which did not resemble childhood.

Schools

I studied at three schools – school with tuition, a parochial school and an ordinary one.

My first school was a special English school at Park Kultury. I passed the interview.

Many years after my childhood, I went to visit my former classmate Lola, now a ballerina at the Bolshoi Theater, and she put on a video cassette. It was a recording of the first day of our first class. A Soviet television cameraman made it for Lola's big-shot father.

It's interesting that Lola was the one I was madly in love with in the first grade. I had a crush on her immediately, as soon as she sat next to me in the lunchroom, she was small, swarthy, with round eyes. "How do they let such little ones in here!" I thought delightedly.

It was a color recording. The first of September 1987. The school yard. The Soviet parents are like children themselves. They are elongated children who have grown in all directions: their faces are naïve and bright. Their offspring look more suitable, the tenderness of their faces matches the miniature nature of their bodies. The principal speaks into the microphone, a woman with an experienced look and red curls. Her voice is filled with power and hysteria at the same time: "Together with our Homeland and the Party the school has begun Perestroika! Recently we began to help the children of Nicaragua!" A bald man in enormous glasses is smoking into his covered palm bashfully.

I see myself, and Lola presses pause.

My parents didn't make it into the film, but there I am. An alien. An alarmed, sensitive face. There are crimson, lavish colors up to my chin. It seems they are flowers – an extension of me, there are circuits in them. Through the flowers I understand the surrounding earthlings in the schoolyard.

Lola presses play again, and we are taken away from the parents....

I remember well how I came to this tall Comsomol girl, who squeezed my hand, and as we walked she repeated:

"Don't be scared of me, don't be scared."

"I'm not scared."

We hurried, the song "Merry Wind" reached us, a warm wind swept through our hair, and there was a sweet anticipation as if beyond the threshold of the school an incredible miracle awaited us. Or rather, numerous miracles, each one more incredible than the next. This was treacherous delight, it seemed that my parents had been left behind forever, and from now on everything would be different.

At the school we went up two flights of stairs, reached the spacious classroom, and I placed a bouquet above a heap of other flowers. The Comsomol girl sat me down at the last desk on the edge, gave me a striped thin book with the title *Bim-bom* and wished me luck, saying: "Study to make Mama happy and your enemies afraid!" And she vanished. I opened the book, and inside were grandpa, grandma and the chicken Ryaba. A chubby boy next to me had a tuft of hair and rosy cheeks. In a muffled voice he dropped into my ear: "Artyom Glukhov".

Alexandra Gavrilovna appeared. My first teacher. From the first glance it was clear that she combined kindness and strictness. She was entirely made up of solemn clumps of wool: the large clump was her body, the smaller one was her head, and the smallest was the grey clump on top of her head. Later I noticed her hands: sickly pink, with snow-white lines from constantly using chalk and wiping it off with a cloth.

"Write down all the words you know!"

Artyom didn't know how to write. I covered the page on both sides. For example, I wrote "old people", for some reason. Evidently I was inspired by the "grandpa and grandma" that I saw in the book.

And again the video cassette fills what has been erased from my memory.

"There is no peace in Lebanon," Alexandra Gavrilovna says with concern, and sighs.

She points to a group of boys by the blackboard:

"Tell me, boys, how do they differ from you?"

Complete silence.

"Red ties!" Comes a piercing voice.

The camera points to a distant corner.

"Stand up, boy. What did you notice, boy?"

I stand up, alarmed.

"They have red ties…."

I say this knowing that I will not have a red tie, Papa won't allow it. Why do I say this? Like a spy, from the first minutes of the Soviet school I want to get inside the system? Or am I moved by the sudden urge to break away from my family and join everyone else? Or can I simply see things clearly and couldn't resist being the first to speak?

"What's your name?"

"Seryozha."

"What's your surname?"

"Shargunov."

The teacher's face changes slightly, and she frowns. She knows whose child I am all right.

I will come to be fond of this teacher, and she will start to look after me when she discovers that I read and write faster and better than the rest. "A golden head," Alexandra Gavrilovna will say as she walks past the blackboard. "Seryozha, you are a lot like Seryozha Gorshkov. He was one of my pupils, the grandson of an admiral!"

She came to the school back in the 1930s. I remember: talking about the war, respectfully, stressing the pauses, she said the name: "Stalin", and an echo was heard.

Now it's embarrassing for me to remember how, from one year to the next, with increasing boldness, I argued with Alexandra Gavrilovna's sermons, and she became increasingly powerless: Perestroika had begun.

In the first grade I still told the story from the textbook about dear Lenin and bullfinches, or about the "society of clean plates" that was organized by Ilich. But in the third grade, I put up my hand, and standing up, mocked the song "Dubinushka", which played from the tape recorder that the teacher turned on, and called Lenin nasty names to the laughter of the class, which had stopped wearing the usual uniforms and was now just dressed in whatever clothes they wanted to. Incidentally, from this diversity it became quite clear who was poor, and who was rich.

In the first grade I was still obedient. In a rounded, important voice, Alexandra Gavrilovna told us that the world was divided. Opening a large book, she showed a photo in which the gold of our wheat was being mown, and a photo of America, where in the smog, under skyscrapers, homeless blacks were sitting. "Russia is the day, America is the night," this was what the teacher taught us, in short.

In the mornings, a cheerful delegation of pioneers sang us songs about the revolution. Their leader, happy and big-cheeked, declared broadly: "And the Tsar only slept on the porch and ate gingerbread!" (the bones of the Tsar's family were already kept at our home at that time).

The pride of the school was also brought to our lessons - a poet from a senior class, a mixture of Pierrot and Duremar. He was probably due to receive a gold medal. He had a blocked-up voice, a hanging nose and a pale face. He shook his head with his long locks and droned: "Lenin is dead, Lenin is dead, Lenin is dead…."

At the music lessons, almost all the boys behaved terribly, snorted and crawled off the chairs, feeling that they were allowed to do anything. Music was taught by a nervous, goggle-eyed woman with black hair cut in a square. Who wouldn't be nervous! For some reason

I pitied her terribly, I even dreamt of her, and I woke up crying. At her lessons I was better, quieter and more musical than all the rest. Three years later she died. From throat cancer.

Grandpa told me
How he served in the Kremlin
How he guarded Lenin's room
With a rifle in his hand.

"Baaaahh," the inveterate hooligan Andrusha Drugov shouts – he resembles a stupid bull, and in reply the nasty Pasha Yekimov laughs – he looks like a boiled sausage, and is the son of a police officer.

The teacher slams her hand on top of the piano with the anger of a fanatic insulted by blasphemy.

Everyone stops talking, and a few obedient voices, mainly girls, continue:

And in the photograph
My grandpa's with the soldiers
Marching with Lenin
With a rifle to the parade….

I didn't do well in the physical education lessons. I couldn't jump over the hobby horse and do pull-ups. I was second-to-last by height, I was short. Then I started to jump and learned to do pull-ups. The last was the wild Tigran, who was little and sinewy, and covered in black hair at the age of seven. He roared in delight and leered at the girls, threw himself at them, embracing them in his small but tight grip…. In the toilet I was shocked to see him, victoriously grinning, not urinating in the toilet, but on the floor, with splashes and spraying….

Our gym teacher, a grey-haired and hoarse old man, who constantly whistled furiously, disliked me most of all: I was poor at physical education at that time. For the sake of honesty, I should note that by the age of 10 I had become one of the three best, although I still didn't get along with the gym teacher, who replaced the former one who had died. The first teacher, while he was still alive, came up to the classroom during the break after my unsuccessful attempts to jump over the hobby horse. He asked about me. He cursed. "But he reads well!" I heard the voice of the fairy, Alexandra Gavrilovna. The wicked man mumbled something and stormed off.

Alexandra Gavrilovna ordered us about calmly and confidently. In the parallel class a relatively young woman was in charge, who was brightly made-up and boiling with fury. We heard her rage – she shouted, stomped, and exploded over the smallest faults. When I saw her in the corridor, I turned away – her gaze, which was disapproving in advance, burned fiercely. Alexandra Gavrilovna made do with gentle but serious persuasion; she used her artistry, and could crush you with a rebuke. Yes, she was an artist. I remember she played a duck – it was a very close resemblance.

The class was without a doubt divided from the very first day. Lola, for example, sat at the first desk, and the film shows how Alexandra Gavrilovna specially looks after the girl, showers her with praise, unable to endure the magic of power. Frowning, Lola's father stands by the door, whose Asian nickname is known to everyone today, the only parent allowed to come to us. The camera constantly captures his stern, set expression.

The school children were not equal. Lola, an oriental little thing, walked next to the blue-eyed Seryozha Skolov. The son of a diplomat, the same height as her, an impudent softie, he constantly hunched over and at the same time looked like a prince. Arkasha was also rich. His lower lip hung down and gleamed, and the corner of his mouth was twisted. Haughty and nasty, this little baron flew by himself from Moscow to New York at the age of nine. At ten he brought a porn magazine to a biology lesson. But in the first grade, Arkasha had a limitless supply of wrappers.

Wrappers were the supreme entertainment, the meaning of school! At the lessons we heard about the evil America, so that at the breaks, sticking to the windowsills, we beat out fists on the colored papers from American chewing gum – if the paper turned over when you hit it, then you got it. The papers, which smelled sweet, and sometimes were sprinkled with fragrant powder from the recent chewing gum, had colored pictures and photos on them.

During a break I was caught near the bathroom by Sasha Malyshev, whom it seemed poverty had awarded with paleness. Charming-looking, the most timid, with transparent fingers he selected pictures from a North Korean magazine: something purple shone, and figure skaters held crimson flags.

"My mother bought me this magazine and cut them out. Do you think it's suitable?" he asked, embarrassed and hopeful.

"Give it a try," I said and went off to continue playing.

Sasha hung around next to our game, clutching the papers in doubt, and no one paid any attention to him, and I also pretended not to notice him. And then he rushed to the window sill, and the children bent over the bright cut-outs that he held out (oh, the moment of triumph for the poor boy!), but the next moment another poor boy, the D pupil Andrei Drugov, shouted with the swiftness of an A student:

"Take your crap away!"

Everyone laughed. Sasha was pushed away with shoving and laughter, he stuffed the papers into his pockets and froze, not sure whether to go away or get closer. All day, at each recess, he bit his lip and hung around next to the fighting. From time to time someone said: "There you are again with your stuff! Don't stop us playing properly!" "No.... I'll play properly too...." he muttered and went completely pale.

The D pupil Andrei also got laughed at, as it happened. "My Mama goes to the factory. My Mama has a pillow," Alexandra Gavrilovna read out his essay to the laughing class. He, a brilliant D student, curly-haired, goggle-eyed, with round nostrils, would be expelled in the second grade – rumor had it that he was transferred to a school for the mentally retarded.

In the first grade, I drew many pictures and glued them on to a long ribbon, creating an entire cartoon. About an alien, who flew into the forest, then went to the city. At the break I was surrounded by children, they twisted the ribbon; some tried to laugh at me and wanted to tear up the drawings, while others supported me. Arkasha, smacking his lips (the businessman in him awoke) offered to buy the entire ribbon for five wrappers with photographs of American football players. But I didn't want the photographs of football players. I gave the ribbon to Lola. She crushed it without ceremony and stuffed it into her bag, and I realized: my work is not destined to live for a single day.

"I had lice," poor Artyom Glukhov told me. "It was nothing; we got rid of them with kerosene after two days. Grandma says: it's the Americans infecting us. They come to school and release lice…."

In 1987, I saw an American woman at the school. We caught sight of her during recess. The fact that she was American and that she had presents for us in a large plastic bag, which she would give us during the lesson, was understood by everyone immediately. But could we wait five minutes? Could we be sure that we would get a worthwhile present? A begging, crushing crowd surrounded the woman. Even then I looked at this in amazement, where children of different incomes came together, and the girls also went wild. "*Oh! No! No,*" a voice came from the crowd. The bag tore apart, and there were cries of joy! Leaving the missionary, they fought over the blue and brown bears, scratching and squealing by her feet. Little bears the size of beans. The blue ones were preferred; they had a more cheerful color.

I didn't join the Octobrists. I was the only one in the history of the school not to do so. This was the will of my father the priest, but my will was also involved here.

"Why weren't you at the reception?" My classmates asked me.

"I was ill."

"Where's your badge?"

"I lost it."

A flock of girls rushed to the teacher:

"Alexandra Gavrilovna, take Seryozha!"

She made some authoritative and evasive reply.

However, in my heart I regretted that I was not at the ceremonial reception, did not go the Lenin hills, and didn't go to the parade on Red Square. But as early as the age of six, the red flag that was given to be in the yard by my friend Vanka and hidden at home among my toys was discovered by my godmother and thrown into the garbage chute amidst a scandal.

I was lured by the forbidden, by the Soviet. But anti-Soviet things – underground books, magazines, radio voices – also attracted me. A dual nature lived within me.

I was the only one without a pioneer's tie in the large group photo of our class 2B. The photo did not stay with me for very long. Looking at it, I put it on the couch, where the grey striped cat Pumka suddenly jumped from off the floor and scratched a piece of the photo off with her paw. I put this piece away somewhere, intending to glue it back, but I couldn't get around to it, and it got lost. And the photograph with a hole in it is still lying somewhere. It's no good to me; the cat destroyed me and another eight children, including Lola.

In the autumn of 1991, in the orphaned music room, we were asked to choose and prepare a "little flame". The girls swept and dusted, and the wind blew through the open window.

On the piano, among the sheet music someone discovered portraits of Lenin, posters with pioneers and one rare black and white photograph: Lenin, cut out of the darkness by light, glowers piercingly right into your heart. Lenin's tie was black, with white dots.

With relief and fury the boys threw themselves on these pieces of paper! They tore them up, squashed them into a ball, threw them around and scattered the fragments on to each other....

I watched, grinning indifferently. Although the girls still objected, and sighed flirtatiously, seeming to be happy about the mess.

"But don't touch the sheet music," Sasha Malyshev mumbled.

"What does it say here, jerk?" Pasha Yekimov shouted, tearing up the entire pile. He began to leaf through the torn-up music, muttering: Yelochka, Cheburashka, Merry Wind... Look, it's about Lenin again, the bastard!" And grimacing, to general laughter, he sang: "And on this photograph / my father with the soldiers / marches with Lenin / and steps into some shit..." He pulled the pile of sheet music by the corner and tore it in two.

The photographs of Lenin got the worst of it: they were crossed out, they had horns and fangs drawn on them, the eyes were scratched out, four-letter words were written on the round forehead, and finally they were stuck to the wall with chewing gum. And the kids spat at them at a distance of several paces, competing to see who could spit the most accurately.

I began to feel uneasy. Pity for the dead music teacher, and this autumn, clearly the last one for the Soviet land, and the disappointment from victory which gave no warmth – all of this mixed into bitterness, it all came rushing out:

"Hey, you! Wait! You... you there! You were Octobrists, weren't you? Pioneers, yes? Were you lying, then? Leave him alone!"

They didn't listen. Swearing and shouting, they spat even more furiously, cheerfully and thickly....

"Hey, that's enough!"

"Sery, are you nuts or something?" The former leader, the handsome blond boy Anton Kozhemayko said, slurping up his spit noisily.

Something broke inside me. I flew to the wall, tore down the picture of Lenin, which was revolting, and dripping foam, threw it away and jumped on to the window sill.

"Are you going to jump?" Sasha Malyshev asked, raising his head in fascination.

The kids grabbed me by the legs. But I still managed to throw the photo out the window.

Swaying slowly, the horrible, desecrated Lenin flew out of this school, and together with it the wind bore away dead leaves.

Our class slowly broke up. New pupils came to replace old ones. In the third grade, Lola went to the ballet academy. Sasha Malyshev was bitten badly by a dog, and he began to study at home. Pasha Yekimov went to a sport school, now's he a cop, like his father. And only the rosy-cheeked Artyom Glukhov, with whom I was seated on the 1st of September with the books "Bim-bom", would study until graduation, if you believe his page on Odnoklassniki social network site. Judging by the photography, he has not changed much over the years – he is just as chubby, pink and tuft-haired as he was on the day when he did not yet know how to write.

I remember the girls, some pretty and some not so pretty. There was Zhenya Merkulova, tall and dull, permanently spoiled in my eyes by the first impression. On the 1st of September 1987, the beanpole stood up and asked mournfully: "Can I go to the bathroom? Do you have any paper?" and her lip moved feverishly. There was the scruffy, feisty but also rather sleepy Vera Sergeeva, the daughter of the school cleaning lady. There is a type of energetic sleepwalkers, with a haze in their eyes and nonsense in their mouths. I went out with this Vera for a while, pretending to be in love, but I actually loved Lola. And I didn't look at the other girls. I loved Lola alone.

I said goodbye to the paid school after the collapse of the USSR. I moved to the recently opened grammar school – my parents decided that it would be better this way. It was located in a courtyard on Ostozhenka, in the basement of and old building. The ceilings were low and the floors were crooked, with linoleum nailed to them.

I walked to the grammar school through courtyards, between the buildings of the preserved old Moscow and through the Moscow of the early 1990s.

The grammar school turned out to be serene, but mad. I immediately made enemies with everyone there –they were children from another parish, and I was a stranger from elsewhere. Also I laughed when they replied in resonant voices at the backboard about Jesus and the sycamore tree, as if they were talking about Lenin and the bullfinches. Although I also had replied to questions about both Lenin and Jesus in my school life. But I did this calmly, without any false gleam in my eyes, without whining pathos, I thought. Every morning began with a short prayer. It was read out by the pupil who the principle/priest pointed to. The day ended with a half-hour prayer.

After the prayer, we were photographed. A color photograph where everyone looks similar, like a large family, evidently because of the intentionally devout faces. And in the center is the head of the family, the satisfied and confident priest with a brown curly beard.

The photograph hung in the corridor together with the schedule of lessons throughout the two years that I studied there.

This priest was kind and lively, gentle of body, voice and gaze. He taught religious education:

"How terrible to offend your brother! We must remember that Christ appears to us in the form of any person. Christ is in everyone. And by offending another person, we offend Christ."

At this lesson, everyone replied clearly and obsequiously. But recess came, we poured out into the yard, I walked away from the grammar school, and my path was blocked. And the firing started. Without any cause. They had agreed amongst themselves – and started firing. All seven of them threw snowballs at me. In my face, at my head! They yelled: "Bastard! Jerk! Satan,", but were afraid of swear words: an additional painful nonsense of theirs. "I threw a piece of ice in his face," yelled Uzlov, goggle-eyed and short-haired. "Don't let him go," the small dark Zhora breathed in excitement.

"Stop! You were all lying! You were lying! At religious education!" I shouted, white from head to foot.

They laughed and intensified the firing.

"I'm your brother! You're hitting Christ!" A snowball as hard as a turnip hit me in the lips.

They probably enjoyed shooting at their miserable, obligatory present.

"Fucking pricks!" I ran at them with my lips broken, fists clenched, with the twisted face of a hoodlum.

They lashed out at me randomly, laughing happily.

At the school there were several good-looking girls, although they were strange, with cold fish eyes and thick braids, and in these braids, in the coils and weaves, you could read the future: many children.

There was an excellent English teacher, with grey stubbly whiskers and a bald match, a firm and tactful gentleman. And there was a deranged teacher of Russian literature, a yellow hysterical old woman, possessed by crazy ideas which she shared with us with pleasure. She talked about urine treatment and that the Virgin Mary looked after Alla Pugacheva. However, she knew the subjects she taught well and was magnificent in her own way. I also remember a big old lady with a face with raspberry spots – in the corridor after the lessons she began to interrogate me: did I observe all the fasts, and when I made some thoughtless reply, he stamped her feet, demanded my school diary, and wrote on it in red ink: "Hasn't been taught to talk to adults!!!" She resembled the lonely psychopathic housewife from the film "Misery"! I also remember in that corridor there was a freckled boy who rolled his eyes and proclaimed: "Anachema!" (he was certain that this was how "Anathema" sounded), and jokingly fell on the linoleum over and over again.

Another flash: the Great fast, a hazy red sun, stinging frost, a procession of school pupils. We tread snow for half a kilometer. We do this every morning. Finally, the bricks of the Zachatievsky Monastery come through, and behind the walls is the ordinary school where we are fed. We have our own food: sauerkraut and buckwheat. We are fed separately from the local schoolchildren after a recent incident when they gave us the finger from the next table, throwing pieces of sausage, and we fought with them – table against table.

After we had breakfast, we went to the monastery church – the Patriarch had come to visit – you couldn't get through the crowd, we stand on the wooden staircase with tramps, beggars and their children. "We ran away from Chechnya, our house burnt down," a man in a shabby coat loudly reports. "Sery, forgive me… that I threw ice at you…" Uzlov whispers and rubs his close-shaven head. The liturgy is over, and Patriarch Alexis walks down the stairs, smiling with merciful subtlety, he beams at us, kisses Uzlov on his freezing head, and after him comes the beaming Archbishop Arseny, robes, guards, and Dim Dimych Vasiliev comes rolling along like a dark ball, the head of the "Memory" society. Oh, the Moscow of 1993….

From our school, incidentally, half of the pupils joined the clergy. I see their beards and gowns on the "Odnoklassniki" site. Two girls became priestesses.

After a couple of years, alas, I was sick of the grammar school. And I transferred to an ordinary school by the Frunzenskaya metro station. I spent most of my school years there. And so I consider it to be my native school.

Shortly after I left the grammar school, there was a fire, caused by a short circuit. At night, when there was no one around. The fire did not make it to the classrooms: the fire brigade came when the alarm went off. But the corridor was burnt. The flames moved across the walls, and of course licked the pious photo.

A BOOK WITHOUT PHOTOGRAPHS

The new school received me in its coarse embraces. There were many children of workers at the rubber factory. Instinctively, I became friends with the real hooligans. I remember you, Gulichev, round and solid, with whiskers growing early. The crested boxer Bakin.... I deployed my ferocious genes. I joined with the ordinary people, although not in everything, not in everything.... The hooligans beat up the weaker kids. I tried to observe honor, and not take part in the terror. Once, walking to school, I joined a boy from the year below us, whose name I didn't even know, all I knew was his nickname, Down. Tall, stooping, undernourished, with glasses, an insect person, he was shuffling along to school so he could hear his nickname again and get a beating.

"They really bother you!" I exclaimed from the depths of my sorrowful soul.

"What's it to me, I'm used to it," he suddenly said in an intelligent voice. "Everything's going to be fine with me. Three years will go by, and I'll enroll in the biology faculty at the Moscow State University...."

I also didn't harass Pimenov, with the nickname "dumpling" (the sadist Rykov, his patron tormentor, broke his leg on the staircase, "dumpling" went to hospital, the bone healed, and he came back to school. Rykov treated "dumpling" like an object he owned. School, you're a prison!) But it was necessary to fight, to constantly prove yourself.

A miserable, anaemic boy with the surname of Ivanov once sat down in my chair and threw my textbooks on to the floor. This was a challenge. The strong boy with blue, desperate squinty eyes got a beating from me. I hit him in the face, as hard as I could, until he cried and his nose started bleeding, to the point of an unconditional capitulation. There was no other way. But there were also wonderful holy types. Korzinin was a wonderful quiet and modest boy. Oh, Korzinin – a mushroom and berry soul. Fyodorov was a fine, crimson-faced good fellow, although at the age of fifteen he drank so much that he didn't recognize his own mother (quite literally).

I bought the trust of the nasty simple boys, the hooligans, by consistent impudence. Firstly, I drank during lessons. I took a can of beer out of my backpack and sipped it when the math teacher turned around. I gave another boy some. After the lessons, the boys and I drank together, almost every day. We smoked in the bathroom. "Aaaa.. Aaa...." a senior pupil nicknamed Fofan taught me to inhale. He was given this nickname because he liked to give fofans, powerful flicks of the finger to the head. Everyone passed the initiation. But I avoided the annoying fingers of this thug. Once, fifteen minutes before the history lesson began he jumped towards me between the desks in the classroom and begged: "Come on, come on, let me hit you!" and breathed heavily. The janitor was cringing in the corner – a large woman called Abuzyarov – with a bucket and mop. "Sort it out," she said unhappily. "Seryozha, let him do it." I didn't let him, and because of this I was beaten up by senior pupils after the end of lessons in the yard. They took off my hat, the monsters, and threw it over the fence. I couldn't find it. What's the point of remembering that... I wasn't a tattletale then, and I'm certainly not now...

So, I bought the trust of the hooligans by my pranks. To win a bet, I smoked in literature class. At the front desk, I threw the lit cigarette into a plastic bucket. There was a scandal. The teacher ran to get the principal. (While she was away, the cigarette was taken out of the bucket and thrown in the toilet by Zinochka, who was in love with me, a golden-haired and dried-up A student.) I wasn't expelled, although I could have been. I was at the top of the class in history, literature and Russian. The principal, a heavy-set, shabby bearded man resembling the playwright Ostrovsky felt kindly towards me.

Once there was a party at the school.

There was a disco in the basement by the gymnasium. The large, short Mila Sarkisyan, nicknamed Zhu-zhu, was dancing. Sarkisyan was always, like a "madame", next to the wayward beauty Olesya, who hooligans would come up to from behind and stick their fingers under her miniskirt. Olesya would shriek and jump away gracefully, she was slender, with the charm of southern beauty. There was gloom and flashes; I drank down vodka with wine. I dance with Yana Savelieva, pointy-nosed and pretty. She had a T-shirt with the American flag on it; the colonial style is everywhere these days. Tanya Bulanova sings in the speakers: "My clear light, write to me…." Ivanushki sing: "And in the sky are clouds, clouds like people…" The lively song fever of the 1990s. With a couple of drunk hooligans, resting on their shoulders, I leave the gloom of the dance floor, we take off our jackets in the chemistry classroom, and go out on to the snowy street. We fall on the ice. At a kiosk we buy a 0.7 liter bottle of vodka. "Now you're a real friend!" Gulichev hugs me. "Wait! Don't hurry! Don't drop the booze!" Bakin catches up with us. Then come flashes. The classroom, food scattered on open desks. "Don't drink, brother," Lyosha Kobyshev says, a serious and reliable guy, one of the best in the class. He eats his sandwich and looks alarmed. Throwing back my head, I pour the bottle into me – glug-glug-glug – and don't feel the taste of vodka. Oblivion. A flash. Darkness. Tanya Bulanova sings. "My clear light…" Again? Someone's lips. A kiss. I stroke long hair. Olesya? Yana? Zinochka? Tanya Bulanova? A flash. A basin. Cold water over my face. A flash. It's cold. Very cold. I stand in the snowstorm, just wearing a sweater, that's clear, it's terribly cold, and I sway. "Seryozha! Seryozha! What's my name?!" I look through the gloom. "You're Lena," I barely pronounce the words. "Lena Gaponenko." A flash. I'm carried home. In people's hands. Past the red letter M. Past the metro. We run across Komsomolsky Prospekt. They run. "Don't drop him," one person yells. "What, you're scared of cars," another asks stupidly. A gap.

After the eighth grade, most of the hooligans left the school.

I remember: it was spring, I went to school, and before me stands the teacher of algebra and geometry, Mikhail Nikolaevich – a little man of culture, who constantly smoked.

"I'd like to talk to you," he stops me and holds me by the arm. "See how many of your friends have left," he gently spoke the words.

"Huh?"

His voice became stern, like a judge:

"Are you sure that you want to keep studying?"

"Yes, I am."

"You may find it difficult; maybe it's not worth tormenting yourself. There are colleges and technical institutes."

So that's what he wants to talk about. Incomplete secondary education, to go to a technical institute and become a mechanic Perhaps it would be for the best, right?

I hardly drank anything at the graduation ceremony, remembering the alcoholic misadventure in winter. We took a boat trip, solemn and uptight. Yes, we were all a bit ashamed of one another, as if we were meeting years later.

We drank champagne on deck, and the Kremlin stretched out before our eyes. "May our children leave tears on the sheets!" Kostyan Senkevich, a wild, disheveled freak raises his plastic cup. His toast offends me. And I remember it. Pasha Sapunov shakes his peaceful oatmeal-colored head. Kostyan will die in seven years on New Year's Eve – he'll be hit by a car on Komsomolsky Prospekt. Pasha Sapunov will die in the army. I remember on that boat, in response to me "Thanks", holding out a cigarette, Pasha bleated out a prediction: "Thanks is no good, you can't spread it on bread..." He was killed in training by Nizhny Novgorod.

I remembered: we returned to school, there was blue twilight, and on the window sill the teacher of "Information and Computer Technology" Leonid Yegorovich was sitting, a sinewy man, and singing, smiling so broadly that his gums were visible: "We wish you luck, luck in this big world…" The next year he would be fired: in a fit of anger he tore the ear of a rude pupil, and faced criminal charges.

The class leader Tatyana Vitalievna, a friendly, calm woman, the political studies teacher, stands with everyone on the school steps, which is sprinkled with poplar fluff. The sun crawls along the tops of the tree and turns the ubiquitous fluff golden. "You dye your hair, don't you?" the statuesque and freckled Vika Dobrovolskaya asks with drunken enthusiasm and removes a piece of fluff from the woman's hair. "Yes, I do," the teacher says peacefully. A few years later she will die of a burst blood vessel in her head. "I just like the dye, I wondered what the brand was," Vika starts to justify herself.

"Tatyana Vitalievna, take it," I give her the camera.

To make sure I didn't get drunk, she gave me an important task: to take her expensive camera with me and take photos. I took about twenty of them. On the boat I almost dropped the camera in the water, then forgot it in the classroom, but I looked after it, and I hold it out to her.

"Did you get anything?"
"I think so."
"Well done," she fixes her hair.
I was wrong: the film was over-exposed.
How did that happen?
God knows.

About You, Girls

In my pre-school childhood, I found film in the yard with my German friend Vanka Mets. There were 10 photographs on it. When I held it up to the light I discovered a naked woman the size of a cockroach. I could make it out, and remembered it, despite my inexperience and the minuteness of the picture.

"Tits in dough!" Vanka sighed, giving a delighted whistle.

He demanded that I burn the film with matches, afraid that the adults would be angry. "It's forbidden, you go to jail for that, maniacs leave this stuff lying around," he said, feverishly sneezing. He was in a hurry, but I wasn't. Before he burned it, I looked at the photos again. And I even held the burning film in my hands, looking through the fire and light, so I burned my fingers.

Fiery loves pass through my entire childhood. Hotly, pitifully, forgetfully I crawled after one and another, whose image blossomed inside me and thrust into my rib cage, like a powerful flower.

The flowers of love were nourished by the immateriality of relations, and vague dreams. My voice resonated purely, my eyes shone with aspiration of miracles, and I wrote poems.

After the first tongue kiss in my late childhood with the peculiar Oksana, I walked around drunk for a week. I couldn't get to sleep, and through the darkness, stretching out my hand, I took a notebook and pencil from off the floor, blindly wrote lines, and poems came into being: flying golden snakes.

We even kissed in rhymes.

"Yetkul..." I murmured, remembering a distant town where a mysterious branch of the family, who were workers, lived.

"Get cool?" The girl replied, and I caught her giggling mouth.

Greedily, with shaking hands I pick loves.

The first was called Aziza. I was four, she was eleven, and her parents rented a dacha by a field, and mine rented one 200 meters away, by a grove. When I saw her swarthy face, I got stuck, like a wasp in baklava. Unable to read and write, I dictated a message to my mother which was supposed to apply to Aziza, I asked her to come to me and become my wife. On a rainy day, with my nose against the glass, I looked at the road which washed away: whether or not the swarthy girl would appear. I waited in vain. And in autumn in Moscow I was told that Aziza's father had died, a carpenter who made a wooden grill for our bathroom. I touched the wood bars, chipped them off, and thought about the lovely dark-browed orphan with hard cheekbones and a reckless laugh that rang out in the summer field as she ran into her father's embrace.

At the age of five, love was forced on me. It's an interesting topic: false love. It was like this: an old lady who lived nearby, selling strawberries advised me to take her squeaky granddaughter Liza as a sweetheart. "If Mama asks: 'Why did you fall in love with her', say: "Because of her braid". I imagined a yellow, fat sausage that hung from the girl's head, and nodded in fear. The prediction came true: at home, to my Mama's question, who evidently had been fooled by the cunning matchmaker, I muttered: "Because of her braid". We spent all summer together, going for walks, with this girl who had been forced on me, and while I was initially indifferent, in the end I believed that she was dear to me. However, I didn't love her, and simply played along with the game that was proposed by adults.

At the age of six, in Moscow, I developed a passion for the dark-haired Galya, who was five years older than me, who was brought along with her sister who was my age, the pale Masha – they both learned music. Quite unlike the peaceful Masha, Galya was mischievous and forward, tall and constantly laughing, with a cunning smile. But she was also thoughtful. I remember: the evening, her long hair lay on her shoulders, I stroke her hair and shoulders, and a prickly electric spark hits me, but I keep stroking. Galina crosses her legs, and her soft, dusky cheeks turn red.

Her father suddenly died – just like Aziza's father – and the cause was even the same: a heart attack. But instead of being a carpenter, he was an opera singer. The sisters, Galya and Masha, did not know about his death, they were prepared for it, they were told that he was away on a business trip, and they constantly asked their mother: "How's our Papa? Will he be coming soon?" I turned away, keeping the secret. But this game did not even entertain me when I was instructed to keep the sisters away, because their mother was crying in the next room, and my father had started the funeral service. I took the girls into the bathroom, turned on the tap, and shouted with deliberate alarm: "Wait, look what I'm going to show you!" and I started jabbing my finger between the bars of the wooden grill: "Look: here it is! Broninosov will come out now. He lives in the water". I was able to distract them with the fantastic Broninosov during the funeral service, but in the evening I developed a fever.

Their mother once photographed the two of us together: the coal tsarevna Galya and me, the greedy gnome, sneaking a glance at the gleam of the coal. The photo was taken with an incredible Japanese camera, the photo came out and in five minutes it developed, I turned it around for another five minutes, glued to the spot, and they took it from me.

For some reason, I remember that Galya went berserk while sitting at the table. In a fit of excitement, she began shaking the salt shaker over a vase with fruit in it. Many years went by, I recently saw Galya, and on my tongue the taste of salty grapes returned. Salty grapes – hello,

Asia! I saw Galya at church on Easter – she has several children, but she was flourishing, with a slender figure. I asked: where is that photo? She didn't remember any photo. "Do you remember pouring salt on the grapes?" "What," she asked with a cunning smile. She said that she played the harp and could give me a music lesson.

I want to return to Lola from the previous chapter again. I saw her in the school basement of the lunch room having breakfast. The little girl, staring with her round brown eyes, ate two glazed cheeses at once, and her cheeks were wonderfully puffed out.

We called each other. I called most often. "Lolik!" a male voice boomed. "It's for you!" It was her father's voice. "He's a minister of sport or something," our teacher Alexandra Gavrilovna informed my mother in a reverential whisper.

And there, in the first grade I once more pretended to fall in love. With a pale girl with a blond thatch of hair, who constantly pulled up her tights. I saw that she got on well with the other girls, and I decided to get closer to Lola through her, and perhaps cause the uppity Lola to become jealous. My false love was called Vera Sergeeva. For two years we were together, despite the laughter this called up, and eventually we were seated at the same desk, and at home I humbly put up with the jokes about my "romance". I put up with everything, loving Lola. Then Lola went away to the ballet academy, and I immediately abandoned Vera.

In memory of Lola, there was a class photograph taken in the assembly hall. There were five girls between us. In front of me was Vera with her udder-like face. Lola is smiling insincerely, but magically. A little robber. She has a comb in her hair. Her eyes are narrowed evilly. It seems she is hiding something. A glazed cheese in her cheek? I already said that the photograph was soon torn by my cat, who jumped on to the couch unluckily. The class was not destroyed completely; even the teacher stands there with her cabbage hairstyle, but ten people from the first row, including us, were erased by the cat's paw.

I met Lola again when we were in our 20s. She was completely different, but quite magnificent – limber and red-lipped. The main thing about her had not changed, and the main thing in a person is the feeling. The feeling from her was still touching and malevolent: a little robber from a fairy-tale, tickling the neck of a deer with a large knife.

At the age of ten, in the summer of 1990 I found myself sitting at a table with the blond girl Yulia in the writers' "house of creativity" by the seaside near Riga. In childhood, I often went with my parents to the holiday spots of Soviet writers, and Yulia came to Latvia with her grandmother, who was very kind and somewhat ironic, a former prisoner of Vorkuta how was now in charge of ticket sales at the Central House of Writers. The Soviet Union was swiftly plummeting, the Latvians were cheerfully rude, and the prose writer Zalygin, the poet Mezhirov, the critic Lakshin and the journalist Chakovsky desperately clanged their spoons in time with the catastrophe. And I fell in love. Now when I look at the photographs that were preserved where we stand by a green stinking pond or the grey sea (even on the photograph it is cold and dirty, br-r), I note that Yulya is somewhat puffed up – a rubber doll. A pretty doll next to me in the photographs.

Large blue eyes, a pink ribbon of a mouth, golden hair tied up in a bun, white and blue dresses, the look of a naïve beggar. And a general puffiness – her face and figure – which is so piquant at the age of eleven (Yulia was a year older than me).

She was quite popular. "Isn't Yulia very pretty?" a boy called Misha whispered in my ear in the darkness of a movie theater, when we got in through the exit for the final credits of a film about Shao Lin. I exposed him the next day at the beach: "One boy asked me..."

"Who? Which one? Tell me, please!" While she tried to get the name out of me, she begged and whined, I felt a strange sweet excitement, which I wanted to prolong and prolong. I gave in: "Misha" – satisfied, she snorted and left me alone, and I felt sad.

Before I arrived, Yulia hung out with the Latvians, particularly the eldest of them, windblown red, the blond Jan: he drove around the dunes on a motorbike, leaving clouds of sand. When I arrived and sat at the same table with her, the fickle Yulia abandoned the Balts and completely switched to me. Now during walks in the park we were attacked from time to time by a gang of Latvian boys. This was a demonstration of protest and jealousy. Jan bared his large teeth "Sharyryr popraaa!" The boys joined in with their jealous leader. It was the most laconic song of a jealous boy (a mixture of adoration and hatred) that I had ever heard. He shouted: "Sharyry popra…" Adjust the spheres! He declared war on the blue eyes – they were too great, adjust them, without looking, hide, blue-eyed one…

Of course, I fought with him, and was beaten easily, with humiliating shoves, accompanied by the hoots of his friends. Another time he met me when I had just been given a transparent water pistol by my father, as a present on my name day. I walked out of the glass door, waving the wonderful weapon. Jan was fiddling with his motorcycle that was lying on its side, raised his dull eyes, and said: "Yulka's a bitch". He reached me in two strides, tore away the toy with his hand that was black with oil and bounded off – in wide, mocking strides. I chased him to the green pond, where he plunged his arm in up to the elbow. "Give it back!" – the Latvian shut my mouth with a powerful spray of stagnant water. And then he stamped on the pistol with a wild jump.

That summer, the flirt Yulia lured me to her. We played "doctor" every day, feeling each other's stomachs. And I also squeezed her breasts carefully every day, which were already starting to form. I remember that she broke a cup in the room, spread her arms out and fell down on to the bed, and lay there for a long five minutes, her face in the blanket, her arms to the side, as if inviting me to hug her, to lie down with her....

She left a week before I did, and in the garden where bushes of tart honeysuckle grew, which stuck to the tongue and the lips, said in a delightfully feeble, questioning voice: "I'm leaving tomorrow... do we need to say goodbye?" What was she inviting me to – a kiss or a declaration of love? How many times did I play back this unfinished scene!

I met Yulia years later. She was sturdy and solid. The manager of an insurance company. We didn't know what to talk about. I remember a dead pig was washed up on the shore of the dirty Baltic Sea. The dead eyes shone in the sun like slides. But what was on those slides? Evidently the future alienation of Yulia and Seryozha.

The next blond girl was called Zhanna. I was in love with her during the summers of 1991 to 1992. Two years in a row, for three months I felt love for her. Zhanna was clumsy, energetic, boyish, and fond of screeching, with front teeth that stuck out.

We were photographed by her father, a party member, before the Emergency Committee. He took a long time to find a background to photograph us against, and for some reason he chose a shop. I never saw the photograph.

We were brought closer together by bike rides. After riding along the dusty village roads, in exhaustion we flung ourselves on to a wooden bench in the tall grass by the railway line, and did not dare to kiss. Childhood flew past in trains.... Sometimes we gathered mushrooms and played badminton. Every evening, before I went to sleep, I imagined Zhannochka lying in bed, and in my mind, I sent a fiery arrow into her tender heart, across the street, over the gardens.

A large heart, pierced with a long arrow, was painted in white on the barn by her dacha, and I guessed whose arrow it was, not doubting whose heart it was.

The next summer I saw my relations with Zhanna in

the light of the television, which showed us soap operas from Latin America which enchanted all of Russia at the time. I identified myself with the best character in the soap opera *No One But You*, who was noble, proud and suntanned, and like him, I wore a white shirt, with the top three buttons opened, like him I smiled with my eyes, and – adopting his mannerism – I passed my tongue under my lip across my gums. It was a shame that I couldn't grow a moustache. I gave the blond Zhanna the role of the heroine, a sultry Mexican woman whom the villain seduces. She was indifferent, it seemed, toward the impudent Maxim (I called him Maximilliano), my enemy at the dacha, we fought each summer: he either grabbed me and beat me, or the other way around.

Yes, yes, only in childhood was I able to fall in love! It was quite over the top, the way that love is portrayed in soap operas. Falling under the power of another person, whom you take to be a bar of gold, you worship, and her every fault makes your love more intense. Life dazzles you, and you are blinded.

In childhood, everything is combined with shame. Shame comes from ignorance, from a lack of confidence. In childhood, when you say goodbye to your loved one, you resign yourself to it – never mind, you didn't run away from your parents to follow her, but you also didn't ask adults to organize a meeting for you on a new territory. I even called Zhanna once in Moscow (burning with shame). And how embarrassed you were when you suggested exchanging telephone numbers! Here it should be noted that in late childhood shame becomes less frequent, because carnal interest becomes stronger. Without doubts and fears, at the age of seven I dialed Lola's number, but at twelve a call to Zhanna cost me a liter of blood, which came rushing to my face.

The cursed and best years of dreams, timidity, desire and failure!

At the age of fifteen, as I left for Paris, I promised Olesya, a strikingly beautiful classmate with the reputation of a slut, that I would bring her back a souvenir.

She boasted in class that Seryozha had promised her a gift. I bought a long object (an iron statue of the Eiffel Tower), and when I came back I walked down the corridor (with the tower in my backpack), and the girl, sitting in the window sill, beamed alluringly with glitter on her lips and mascaraed eyes.

"Hi!" An oily smile. "How was Paris, then?"

"Fine. Excuse me, I'll go and see the boys…"

I'm still ashamed about my pathetic embarrassment!

Although I also have a relative justification for this: I was afraid to make the class laugh, because of all the girls whom I had chosen to give a present was a slut.

And after that there was plenty of flesh. Meetings at school, on the street, at university and in clubs. But I forgot how to love after the first time in bed. The dawn broke into the room, drowning it up to the tall ceiling, and poetry died, the voice became rough, and the vision gained clarity.

Once I had a girl called Anya. She was smart and nasty, with large fiery eyes, a dark wave of hair, and prominent cheek bones. She was still a student, twenty-one, and by that time I had graduated, I was twenty-two, when we met. We both studied at the journalism faculty, but life brought us together outside the faculty. At the first meeting, we walked over a glass bridge over the Moscow River in March, which had broken up in the sun and looked like mush. We ate tasteless strawberries out of a bag that I had bought. Anya dropped the bag, and it was swept into the mush….

And the endless mating game began between two animals who suited each other very well. We also married playfully, carelessly, in the middle of a drinking bout.

We lived together for several years, pushing each other away hissing and once more coming together in furious tenderness.

We also came together in anger…. This is especially wonderful and prickly – suddenly after exchanging insults, without making up, you look at each other and drop each other, exchanging wet kisses....

Blind, you rudely and brazenly fumble with your hands, and whisper delightedly, like in childhood:

"Tits in dough!"

Grandma And The Journalism Faculty

At the age of seventeen I became an international specialist at the journalism faculty of the Moscow State University – a closed order where only boys could enroll, and only Muscovites.

In 1997, my ancient grandmother came to stay with us from Yekaterinburg, sent by Uncle Gena. She would live with us until her death.

Grandma told me about the village in the Vyatka taiga. My great-grandfather, Alexei Akimovich, a fisherman, covered everything he ate with coarse salt, like frost. In the First World War, he was taken prisoner, but finally returned from Germany to his native hut and to his wife, my grandmother Lukerya Feofilaktovna. In old age, when his legs were paralyzed, the thing that upset him the most was that he could not fish – and he crawled to the river in tears. Grandma talked about sorcery, a curse, envy and jealousy, lover and friendship, the animals, the land, and the way the wine used to be:

"I drank a gulp, and that was enough. I was happy, I'd dance madly! We lived in a friendly way, we gathered in the evenings and sang. When the men grew scarce, we'd put on the harness ourselves and go to the fields, and pull.... When we ran out of energy, we'd sit on the grass, one woman would sing, and another would join in. You'd look around and see a ready choir, we sang together – all the women....

She said that my grandfather, Ivan Ivanovich, an officer and Communist, secretly revered God.

"We'd get into bed at night, and he'd say: 'It's a holiday today, we can't, and turn away.... And when he went away to war, I sewed a prayer for him – "He that dwelleth in the secret place"....

Grandma had only spent two years at school, but she passionately wrote letters to her relatives. She did not put the pen down until she finished the letter. With mistakes, with words that she understood in her own way, but with fiery words she wrote several pages in half an hour.

To start with, when she had just arrived, she asked:

"Seryozhenka, where are you studying?"

"At the journalism faculty."

"At the journal?"

The old three-story building of Moscow University reminded me of an enormous greenhouse. We studied under a glass dome.

At the journalism faculty there were a lot of fashionable kids in enormous boots, shapeless pants with a dozen pockets, glasses without any correction and orange hair. Many of them drove up in luxury cars. The squeal of breaks and skid of tires could be heard every morning.

There were also geeks, usually modest and ugly, always with books – they stuck together.

There were hoodlums too. They hung around in the yard all the time, by the statue of Lomonosov, where they smoked dope and played hackey sack: a miserable bunch of fabric flew from one foot to another.

It was funny that here, like in the Soviet school once, where everyone had red ties put on, I was lonely. Under this glass dome, in my group, at my faculty, throughout the whole year everyone had an identical mood: they rejoiced to meet the times.

Here, in the old building opposite the Kremlin, everything was quite OK.

And this general "OK" rhymed with the word "lonely".

Once I was sitting with my fellow students in the smoking room, which we called "Santa Barbara". (We called it this because the archway entrance resembled the opening titles of the soap opera).

"I heard something: Sour ...." The excited Tolyan said, not without envy.

Kesha, a young man with an ashen face and a pale crooked grin, spat his cigarette out on to the floor.

"What are you doing!" The cleaning lady came running up.

Nimble, dry, in a grey gown, from early in the morning until late she scurried about the journalism faculty battling dirt. She managed to clean all three floors in the faculty.

"What are you doing!" she reached for the cigarette butt. "Aren't you ashamed to litter! There's a place to throw them away!"

Kesha stepped on the cigarette butt, and her fingers hit the rainbow nose of his "Grinders" boot.

"What are you doing?" She raised her eyes.

Kesha took out a new cigarette:

"Take a whole one! It's my treat!"

The old lady fought with the boot, moving it in different directions, but she couldn't lift it up, Kesha's foot was firmly placed on the cigarette butt.

"She likes you," he was given a nudge by Petka, the youngest of us, a blond boy in a leather jacket.

"I'm sick of this," Kesha stopped grinning. "Maybe I can cure your eyes?" He waved the burning cigarette in the old lady's face.

The cigarette went back and forth and made loop the loops, like a plane at a military show.

The cleaning lady bent down. She muttered something angrily and unclear, as if in a foreign language, she went to the bathroom, from where she returned with a bucket, and started cleaning the stall door with a rag. The inscription "toujours fuck" was written in pink on the door – some wit had mixed French and English.

I regret that I didn't intervene in any of this. To my shame, I was dumbstruck.

Everyone got up.

The cleaning lady, not turning her head, carefully erased the inscription. The dirty water ran down the stall door.

In the evening I told Grandma all about it.

"You should have given him what was coming to him! Grandson, don't shake his hand again. He's not a friend to you, he's a bastard."

I directly obeyed Grandma: although I still talked to Kesha, and went to smoke with him, and exchanged phrases, every time I avoided shaking his hand.

In general, there weren't any total bastards at the journalism faculty. Everyone was quite charming and inclined to be kind. But everyone was brought together by their infantilism. An infantile person can be incredibly vile and at the same time extremely subtle, now and then. Kesha – the son of a prominent surgeon – turned around at a lesson on classical literature, and whispered: "What are you laughing at, morons!" and listened with a reverence that even seemed vulgar to me. He played the piano wonderfully, and had been learning since he was a child, and told us about a parrot that he took to clinics, could not save and buried in the garden.

In the evenings, Grandma talked about her life. Her first husband beat her, her father-in-law forced her to sell apples at the train station, and it was at this station that her brother met her by accident and took her back to the village to her father and mother, and there her young neighbor Ivan Ivanovich, whom she had known since childhood, had just lost his wife: she had drunk horse hair along with water from the stream and died in agony. After Ivan Ivanovich was killed on the frontline, Grandma was left with three children, two boys and a girl. She worked in the fields with the other women, buried her fisherman father and took her children to her mother to the Urals town of Yetkul, to her relatives, where she found a job as a laundrywoman at a hotel.

In the war, Anna Alexeyevna saw all four of her brothers die, and her husband Ivan Ivanovich also had four brothers who died, he was the fifth.

"If I had been taught to read and write, I would have been a big boss! I found a place in the world for all my children. My sons – Genka, the head of forestry in the Urals, and your father is a priest in Moscow. People like them! And people would have liked me even more than them!"

"Me? I could have written those... poems. Listen! "I feel so sad, Seryozha, / I only want to die / I'll gulp it down at once / As if from off a spoon..."

"My dear Grandma! You're still young!"

"Young," she shook her head, laughing bitterly. "What are you going on about?"

Her jaw muscles moved under her yellow skin, her grey eyes looked questioningly, and a brown comb held up her grey hair.

I told her everything that had happened during the day. She was my refuge, mysterious, in the forest, and perhaps she answered laconically and simply, but I gathered my efforts to go under the glass dome again tomorrow.

"They don't like the people," I told her.

"The people don't like them either," she chuckled.

"They take drugs."

"Schmugs, I heard about that. What about you?"

"No, never."

"You'll be a poor fool."

Once I brought home a newspaper with poems in it, with my photo on the page.

"Is that you?" Grandma was amazed. "Bend down: I want to whisper something..."

I obediently leaned over.

"If you have a child, don't put him in the newspaper, keep him out of it. Only after he turns five. Little children are not protected from curses."

After the first "A" at the winter exams, Grandma forced me to take a banknote from her pension – she kept money in a little table by the bed, which had a large scarf tied around it.

She pushed this note into my hand with such a prayer that I could not refuse.

I also read the homework out loud: Old Russian and classical literature, and stories in English.

She listened in exhaustion. Although she listened to the old Russian chronicle with Kii, Shchek, Khoriv and their sister Lybyd quite enthusiastically, turning her ear and often blinking, as this was a part of life that she had personally lived through and was quite familiar with.

When the reading ended, she sat on the bed: she slid her feet in woolen socks into her slippers, by touch, and took a prayer book, a fat book which was covered in stains from medicine and food. She swallowed the prayers, constantly moving her cheek bones.

"If only death would come," she said again.

Without replying, I went to heat up the supper (my parents were absent), and suddenly there was a crash. I ran into the room.

"What's that? What's that?" Grandma asked capriciously.

The light fitting had fallen on to the floor by her feet, and her slippers were sprinkled with tiny fragments.

Since then, every time that Grandma called for death to come, I teasingly interrupted her and objected. "If I don't say anything, she really will die," I thought in alarm.

Soon after the incident in the "Santa Barbara" smoking room, I witnessed the sequel.

It all took place at the bottom of the steps inside the faculty, by the entrance, which was usually crowded.

I was sitting around with the guy drinking beer.

Suddenly the cleaning lady appeared. She pointed her finger:

"That's him!"

A figure in camouflage clothes lumbered towards us: the guard of the journalism faculty.

"What's the problem?" Kesha put the bottle down.

"Hit him, Nikitich!" The old lady cried. "He's the one!"

The man grabbed him by the ear, and pulled him outside. The students watched, chatting among themselves, and no one moved. Only a few of us, his classmates, and the cleaning lady followed.

The man let Kesha's ear go and dragged him by his bright lilac sweater

"Does that hurt, you piece of crap? Why did you offend a working person?"

"I won't do it again," Kesha whined.

"There!" His rubber boot gave a kick, and the student went flying off the stone porch, into the bushes, on to the ground.

"Not enough?" the man turned to us.

He smelled of onions.

A month later, on the same porch, in my presence he happily informed the professor of Russian literature Tatarinova:

"There are my onions! I plant them on the windowsill. I don't need flowers, you can't eat them…"

She sighed and flirtatiously adjusted her hat.

He always wore the same things: camouflage pants and a jacket, with a black singlet under his jacket, and rubber boots on his feet.

Since then, we didn't offend the cleaning lady, and even started to be afraid of her.

But we did begin to pay some nasty attention to the guard. Kesha and several of his friends began to mock him quietly. When they walked past the table, they would drop cigarette butts, seemingly by accident. Some bold guys crept behind him and poured Coca-Cola under his chair. They shouted: "Yuck, he's pissed himself!" "Don't beat me! Protect me!", "Shell-shocked!"

The man sat for hours in his camouflage uniform at an old Soviet table.

"Why are you making all that noise?" he got up, not understanding, and clenched his fists.

He had a habit: several times a day he would stand by the door and furiously check the student IDs.

"Where's the photograph?" He stopped a third-year student who looked like a baby camel, a journalist at a popular newspaper.

"It came unstuck."

"I can't let you in."

"Here's my journalist ID."

"I don't know anything about that. It came unstuck…"

"Maybe your moustache came unstuck?" the journalist suggested.

"Why is that?"

"Maybe you're Hitler?"

After five minutes of arguing the student was allowed in, but now, when he walked past the guard, every time he said in his mocking voice:

"Hi, Adolf!"

And he hurried off.

I talked to my grandmother about the war a lot.

"It was terrible – all my brothers were sent to war. My husband was taken away. It was all his fault – the scum. How could such a person be born! How many people curse him!"

"Who, Granny?"

"Adolf."

"Did you see him?"

"As if I needed to …"

Obeying an incomprehensible urge, I brought a history book into her room with pictures of Hitler, among others.

She took the book, looked at it attentively, and suddenly, with a yellow fingernail, she began scratching at the photographs, shredding the paper.

"Granny, what are you doing?"

"He's a murderer, damn him. He killed my husband."

The bullet hit Ivan right in the heart.

According to the recollections of a man in his division, he went into the attack with the photo of his young son, my father, attached to his chest, over his coat. The bullet went through the photograph.

My father, who was three, was playing in the hut, on the floor, at the time. Suddenly he cried and shouted:

"Daddy's been killed! Daddy's been killed!"

He was beaten, tore himself away and cried:

"But it's not my fault, it's not my fault that daddy's been killed!"

In winter, Grandma fell over in the corridor. I lifted her up, she was light, and put her on the bed. My parents called the ambulance. I sat by her, holding her by the hand, the old pulse beat intensely, Grandma whined quietly, while I said nothing and kept hoping that she had not broken something.

The ambulance arrived, and the doctor said she had probably broken something. Grandma had to be carried carefully, on a chair. Slowly and carefully I put Grandma on a chair. I wrapped her in a fur coat, in a white woolen scarf, and gently (but she still groaned) I pulled on her fur boots.

I tied her to the chair with shirts and tights. Together with the guy from the ambulance, we carried her. In her room, her black crutch stayed in the corner, with a guilty look.

"Don't shake me, dears," Anna Alexeyevna cried without tears.

We put her into the elevator.

Off we went. On one floor our neighbor came in, a girl of an uncertain age.

She saw Grandma and snorted, and gave me a flirtatious look of solidarity.

Her eyes ironically widened, as if to say: "Oh, these old people."

"Idiot," I scowled, and turned away.

Grandma, not holding anyone's gaze, wildly moved her eyes.

We drove through Moscow at night, the lights licked grandma's face with its high cheekbones, and her jaw bones moved insatiably and strangely.

After the hospital, where she was X-rayed (a hip fracture), I took Grandma to the dacha. There she began to move, using an iron walker, and lived several more years.

The cosmic night floods into my heart when I think of your death, Grandma.

Anna Alexeyevna died at the age of 92 after New Year, before the Russian Christmas. She ate the festive food and drank wine ("Terribly sweet!") When it came to food, Grandma, like a primitive, was original, combining things that could not be combined: she ate chicken with chocolates, aubergine paste with bananas, and herring with biscuits.

Before she died, in the evening, from her bed she firmly pressed my arm with her two hands. As if she were saying goodbye. "Move the chairs. At night I run into them, I don't know where I am. Goodbye, goodbye, my dear companion!" And shook my hand.

During the night, Grandma had a stroke. She lay unconscious for two days and then passed away. I kissed her cold cheek, her grey eye reflected the winter window, her frame resembling a cross, which was roughly insulated with cotton wool and plasters. Grandma was buried in the village of Mogiltsy in the Moscow Region, not far from the house where she died.

A week after the funeral, empting the garbage pail into the container at the end of the street at the dacha, I suddenly saw with horror several rags that resembled Grandma's clothes. "That's quite an ordinary matter," I said to myself. "A person dies, and some of their things are thrown away." But then I saw the comb. Brown, having served Grandma for several years, and which became close and mysterious for me, it lay among the trash. In the piercing winter wind, the grey hairs between the teeth of the comb fluttered, came to life and murmured. Grandma's hair. I grabbed the comb from out of the trash, and frantically kissed it.

In the summer of 2002, after Russia lost to Japan, a crowd of football fans rioted on Manezh Square. The enraged kids from the outskirts of the city destroyed and defaced everything around them: they smashed shop windows, turned cars over and set fire to them. And at this time, in the courtyard of the journalism faculty (it was closed on the summer Sunday) a group of students were hanging out. They were playing hackey sack and laughing. They didn't pay attention to the world around them – the hubbub, crashing and smoke that was coming from Manezh Square. And only when a noise was heard on the other side of the fence (a policeman came running in a torn shirt, with a gang of half-naked savages chasing him), did the students stopped their game. In a minute, the street was filled with a crowd. They were rolling a car over. The students galloped like a herd of roe deer, rushing to the faculty doors. They frantically rang the doorbell. No one opened up. Meanwhile, as was only to be expected, a few fans were breaking through the gates with iron bars.... They ran over to the cars and started bashing in the bumpers and windows. The students didn't even think of protecting their property.

The latch rattled.

A gloomy man in camouflage clothes stood in the doorway.

"What do you want?" He yawned: he smelled of onions and heavy sleep.

"We study here!" Kesha shouted.

"I know you, don't I?" The guard got out of the way, letting them in.

And he slammed the door.

On that day, seven of the cars parked in the yard were vandalized.

That summer I received my diploma.

The Bolbases

It was Bolbas who gave me the idea to go into politics.

He didn't come out in the photo on my cell phone. His wife didn't get into the picture at all. You can see his coat and his tall fur hat. Instead of a face, a pink blur. I deleted this photo on the day that I took it.

On the last visit from Uncle Kolya I had already made it into literature. I had received two prizes, and had three books published.

On one of the moments in the morning when he was still sober, and so especially gloomy, Uncle Kolya said to me, loudly leafing through "Novy Mir", unable to find my story, which was hidden in the middle, and so getting even more angry:

"You write and write… Scribbling is fine. But you should help the people with a cause."

"How?" I asked.

"How, Shmow," he mocked me. "Did you hear about the monetization? We've been deprived of the last thing we had. Old people have gone out on to the streets. And where are you? Writers…. If you had your own team, you would go out too. You'd travel around the country and talk to the people. You know how -they'd respect you!"

"And what should it be called?"

"Hooray," said Kolya.

"Hooray?"

"Well, that's what your book is called. I haven't read it, but I can see it on the shelf. But the name is suitable. It's short and clear. And easy to shout."

This was the legacy Uncle Kolya left to me on his last visit….

In my childhood, Uncle Kolya used to visit several

times a year. His appearance was simultaneously kind and impressive. He worked as the head of a workshop at a metallurgy factory in the Ural city of Orsk. Kolya's surname was Bolbas, which was quite suitable for him – powerful and funny. He was a pink-faced man, with blue eyes, a snub-nosed blond with heavy fists and a barrel of a stomach.

I remembered Bolbas in a shirt unbuttoned to his belly button, exuding heat. He sat there, quite glorious, and picked his large nostril. I looked at him with eyes wide-open, as if he were an animal. Hairs stuck out of the depth of his nostril. His blue eyes focused on me, and he smiled tenderly. Kolya had something that natural people in Russia have – charm. He could pick his nose, but just by his presence he inspired appetite, he smelled of sweat, but for some reason this smell was comforting.

Bolbas never visited empty-handed.

A fisherman, hunter and bee-keeper, he would bring a catfish, a boar leg, or a weighty lump of honey. I remembered the catfish clearly, because they resembled each other: Uncle Kolya and the catfish.

The factory with incandescent, clanking steel did not fit with the torpid, coarse Bolbas. Kolya really did look sleepy during the day. He came alive at night: he walked heavily from the room to the kitchen, opened the cupboards with a squeak, banged the fridge door, rattled the pans, poured water, and started boiling and frying. He ate at night, and during the day he rested, snoring (a frightening hr-r, a moaning pi-i) with his bare stomach facing up. He woke up my parents at night, and Mama taught me to wake him up during the day. I brought the cat to him and threw it mercilessly on to his stomach, or I rang a bell next to his ear, or beat the massive buckle of his belt against the floor. The snoring stopped, uncle shook all over and groaning, looked around in fright. If it was the cat, he would pass his hand over its back, pick it up by the scruff of the neck and throw it on the floor. If he noticed me, he would ask hoarsely:

"What are you making that noise for, boy?" and go back to sleep.

What kind of uncle was he to me?

Kolya and my Papa grew up together. His mother was my grandfather's sister (whose maiden name was Shargunova). All four of her brothers were killed in the war. And her husband was also killed in the first months of the war, a farm boy, who left her with a baby boy and the funny surname Bolbas, which resembled a man's pot-belly, whose baby boy would grow many years later. Kolya's widowed mother sheltered my grandmother, also a widow, with three children, in the Ural town of Yetkul, where she went from a Vyatka village. Kolya's mother worked as a saleswoman in a shop, and my grandmother found a job as a laundrywoman at a hotel.

My grandmother introduced Kolya to his future wife, a girl from Orenburg who stayed at the hotel. Kolya's local girl didn't go to the movies with him, and my grandmother sent her guest to go with him. They watched *The Cranes Are Flying*. He took her back to the hotel, and the next day he came for her again. He abandoned his former girlfriend, and fell so in love with the new one that she soon had to say goodbye to Orenburg – they got married a month after they met.

Anna, Kolya's wife, was a seamstress by profession, a dark-haired, cheerful and simple-hearted girl of ample proportions, and came to us with him before they flew to Cuba. I was seven years old. From the grey industrial Orsk to the blue ocean, the country sent Kolya to build a factory. A grown-up daughter remained in Orsk.

Anya often recalled the story of how she met Kolya. With gentle irony and a tender smile he backed up her memories. "How well it began with us! He took me to a film, and on the way back he sang songs. You'll sing me all the songs that there are while we walk. We walked until it got dark. And how did you get the first kiss from me? You kneeled before me! What are you laughing for?

And how you begged me to marry you? You said: you'll bathe in honey, Anyuta, I'll do everything for you, live with me and be glad you are the way you are. Is that what you said? That's right, you're nodding. And when you found out that I was expecting Tanyushka, you jumped up to the ceiling for a whole hour, the neighbors called the police, they thought we were having a fight."

Every evening and every morning, on the days when the Bolbases stayed with us, the same thing repeated itself: I plunged my fist into Kolya's fat stomach with all my might, as if hoping to release air from it.

Auntie Anya reprimanded me in alarm, but even so, in the mornings and evenings, the potbelly rolled around the room. Uncle said bravely: "Go on, hit me! Do you think I'm afraid? It's not fat, it's muscle!" I would hesitate, and he would yawn indifferently, and mutter: "Go on, kill me, don't put it off", and chuckle as if he was joking, and I would turn away or talk about something else, and suddenly hit him hard. Bolbas frowned.

"Are you alive?" his wife asked with worry.

"I'm OK."

"Seryozha's doing the right thing: it's high time you lost weight, see what you look like!"

"In my youth I could do a handstand on rings." Laughing, he stroked his belly, and his face shone: the punishment from a child was over.

He talked quietly in general, laughing. Why raise your voice when you have such a big body?

"Uncle Kolya, what's it like at the factory?" I asked.

"Fine. Do you want to go to the factory?"

"Aha."

"You can't just go there straight away." And he started to explain things to me in his unhurried, slightly mocking manner. "You need preparation. Cosmonauts have to be prepared to go into space, and you also need to prepare for the factory. To fight wall to wall, to ride on the roof of a train, to encounter a bear in the forest and run away unharmed. What else?" he pursed his lips and blew both disdainfully and gently, as if he was blowing away fluff. "And you need to know how to use the equipment."

"Have you seen all of that?"

"I've experienced it. Ask your father. He's also a factory man. After the Suvorov academy he poured steel at the factory. It was later that he began to have poems printed and moved to Moscow, and came to believe in God."

"Do you like the factory?"

"It's fine. It's hard, but I can't live without work. The guys like me."

"The robots?"

"The guys. My comrades. There are lots of people. It's hot and stuff. It's noisy. Sparks fly. I'm telling you: you need to be prepared for this from an early age. A friend of mine nodded off and his arm was crushed."

"How do you mean it was crushed?"

"Up to the shoulder," Bolbas said unflappably and patted his sturdy shoulder. "He was given a trip to the Crimea, but what was the point. He wasn't going to grow a new one."

How did it happen that on that day I went with Auntie Anya to the market by trolleybus, was sitting by the entrance, turned around, waving my arms, and the door opened and slammed on my right hand. It squashed it painfully. I couldn't pull it back. Perhaps this was retribution for the fist that I rammed into my relative's belly?

Auntie Anya snivelled, rushed to the driver's compartment, the doors closed, the people going in and out cursed, but my hand was free.

"Don't fool around!" Auntie Anya said, feeling the bones of my fingers. "Are you alive?"

"It's not me. He can't drive. I pointed at the driver's compartment. "Country bumpkin!"

"What?" She recoiled.

"What is it?" When I saw the expression on her face, I was more frightened than when the iron door closed on my hand.

"Country bumpkin…" She said. "Have you ever been there?"

"Where?" I asked in an injured voice.

"Where, where… Where your father was born. Where Uncle Kolya comes from. Where all of our people are from. Never say: country bumpkin, you get it?"

I nodded, embarrassed by the passengers around me, and imaging that I had said something quite terrible.

"I'm going to leave you now. Safe journey, city slicker!"

"Don't leave me."

The trolleybus stopped. Like a shadow, not feeling the bruise, I ran after her.

"We're going to the market. And what's at the market? That's where the country bumpkins are. A lot of people have insulted the countryside. And now you have. But the countryside gives us food and drink, milk, butter, cheese, cottage cheese, meat. Where do you think it's from?"

"Apples, pears, pumpkins…." I joined in energetically, trying to smooth over my guilt. "Feijoas!"

"Feijoas came from a different countryside, not Russia. But also the countryside. How's your hand? Is it better, you idiot?" By her intonation I realized that I had been forgiven.

It's strange: over twenty years have gone by, but I still get terribly distraught if I hear the disdainful words "country bumpkin" or the patronizing "country". I freeze and my cheek starts to twitch, and my right hand starts to ache – because this is not right, it's impossible, it's forbidden. Otherwise Anya Bolbas will lunge at you in a trolleybus in the middle of town.

They were holy people, Kolya and Anya, who were never unfaithful to each other and never felt the urge to be unfaithful, as they both told me separately, when I was an adult. On temperamental Cuba, nothing shook their virtuous union.

However, Kolya drank a lot of rum with his fellow countrymen, and also with Blacks and Latinos, and learned several of the local songs, which they bellowed, hugging each other, and he amusingly distorted them to sound like Russian – the result was a preposterous collection of words in the style of futurism, but history has not preserved the words. Congratulations came from Cuba on holidays: I remember a furry hologram a monkey, parrot and coconut danced if you moved the postcard back and forth, and I also remember a photograph placed in the envelope – the coastline seen from the plane, the place of residence of the Bolbases, and the nearby place where Uncle Kolya worked were marked with crosses in ballpoint pen.

The Bolbases left in 1987 and returned in 1990. They brought pineapples and coconuts, sun eaten into their skin and the belief that life was getting better. During his years of work, Uncle Kolya had received quite a lot of certificates, and now they could buy a new apartment, a car, and help their daughter. From the impressions of Cuba, Anya could not forget the "cucaracha" – large flying cockroaches that astounded her. Uncle Kolya sang a few Cuban songs that he had translated into Russian, and in the morning he went to a rally on Manezh Square, saw Yeltsin and returned with a pile of newspapers, and until late at night the Bolbases sat with my parents, in heated discussion. Uncle Kolya promised my father that when he got to Orsk, he would leave the party, and also discussed the "strong manager" who "would like to be a man of the people, but is not allowed to", and about their ancestors who had perished: "half of them were unmasked as kulaks, and half were killed on the frontline". His usually slow and gentle speech became somewhat thicker, and slogans could be heard booming from the kitchen.

At the end of the year, freedom triumphed, and the Bolbases' "Cuban certificates" were annulled.

In the mid 90s, Uncle Kolya left the plant – they stopped paying. The Bolbases now fed themselves thanks to their extensive country apiary, and did not come to Moscow. I heard news about their lives. Their daughter had given birth to a daughter of her own, and got divorced. "Kolya drinks a bottle of vodka over a meal," my uncle Gennady from Yekaterinburg reported regretfully.

The next meeting took place in the winter of 2004. The Bolbases gathered their efforts and came to Moscow. I met them at the train station. As I approached, I trained my cell phone on them and took a photograph. The photo didn't turn out well, it was one to delete. Kolya stood on the platform, enormous, in a tall fur hat, with a wide red face, from which the Cuban tan had not yet vanished, it seemed, but on his cheeks, like frost, there was pale stubble. He stood there and did not move, waiting for me to come to him. I kissed his cheek, feeling the prickles, and kissed Auntie Anya: she hadn't changed at all, only developed a middle-age spread, and resembled a domestic duck. Her dark bird's eyes had a peevish look, I noticed at once.

I pulled a suitcase with one hand, and in the other I held my large, heavy-set relative by his elbow, who like a snowman, slid along the platform, risking falling to pieces.

I brought the Bolbases to my parents, where Uncle Kolya proceeded to fill himself with vodka.

"My tormentor! You've ruined my whole life!" Auntie Anya sighed.

He frowned, and with a feeble woman's voice, he began swearing at her. My father, the priest, got up from the table, and my parents, asking me to stay with the Bolbases for a week, quickly went away to the dacha. Uncle Kolya drank the whole time and swore at his wife. At dawn I could already hear him coughing and his furious, powerless swearing, and Auntie Anya would reply, offended: "What are you bothering me for?" She constantly sighed about her ruined life, and that in

Moscow they needed a doctor (to examine her husband) and a lawyer (to receive compensation for the worthless certificates).

I took Kolya to a good doctor I knew, but it all ended with the patient swearing at him. "He has no idea about anything. He didn't even take a proper look at me. In our city we have Klavdiev, a therapist, hands of gold, he cured my hernia, but here..." Pursing her lips and piecing me with a condemning look, Anna listened to her husband. Things didn't work out with the lawyer either: he turned out to be an ignoramus, as he said it was pointless to hope for compensation.

Filled with vodka, Uncle Kolya revived his childhood: he swung a scythe in the fields... He said that he did everything conscientiously. "And what do I have from that? Wretched lungs. Hear how I cough, that's from the factory air." The Bolbases didn't mention Cuba – their ruined hopes were connected with it.

Once when I came home in the evening, I was greeted by numerous dumplings, fatty and greasy, which they had spent half the day making, obviously swearing at each other as they did so.

"Eat up, boy, we're kind," Uncle Kolya winked at me with his blue eyes. "Would I leave my relatives without food?"

I ate five of them, and didn't want anymore, and the Bolbases got offended: they stopped talking to me, they pretended not to hear me, and exchanged a short sullen phrase with aristocratic gallantry. Offended at me, they stopped swearing at each other.

But half an hour later, Uncle Kolya looked into my room, apologizing, with a timid, vague smile: "Shall we have some pelmeni?" Then a harsh cough wiped the smile off his face. I said I didn't want any. "Give me 200 rubles," he said through his cough. I gave him 1,000, I didn't have anything smaller, and my relative went out, then came back (although he could barely move). He didn't give me any change, and soon his angry swearing could be heard all through the apartment.

"Do you have friends?" Uncle Kolya asked me over a pelmeni breakfast.

"Yes."

"Where do you drink?"

"At cafés."

"That costs so much money!" Auntie Anya exclaimed tearfully from the stove.

"My idiot wife has been bothering me: take me to a restaurant. You used to, she says. We have a café by our house. I went in and sat down. "Pour me some beer," I said. So the girl brings me a mug, and then gives me the bill. My eyes popped out of my head. That was for three gulps of beer. Back home I said to my wife: "No, there won't be any restaurants for you!" He banged his fist on the table. "Never, none…"

Auntie Anya silently bent over the stove, as the pan sizzled.

Two years later he died.

Auntie Anya moved in with her daughter and granddaughter in the town of Ozersk, which is closed to this day, with a deep lake with abundant vegetation and radiation. She visited Moscow again, and I met her at the train station, and she lived at my parents' dacha for a month. It was summer, and in the evenings she went to visit the neighbors who had a beehive. "I look at the bees as they move, and I remember my Kolya. He kept an apiary until the very end…" She would take one bee every visit, and removing her clothes, stick it in her side or in one of her buttocks. The bee would crawl around on the ground, dying. The old lady nimbly took out the sting. But in these evening sessions of folk medicine – the stings supposedly helped with blood pressure – I saw something pagan: through pain she mourned for her beekeeper husband, letting blood in memory of him….

When I saw Auntie Anya off to the train, I took her to the station café and ordered fried salmon and beer.

"What an interesting fish! And where does this beer come from? Germany? When I go home I'll tell them how Seryozhka treated me in Moscow…"

She drank half a mug and said

"You know, I probably should have let him drink."

"Uncle Kolya?"

"Yes."

"He was the one who pushed me into politics."

"What are you saying?"

"He said: create a movement. And people will join it."

"And did people join it?"

"How should I put it…"

"You should listen to Uncle Kolya more. He could have given you such advice. I'm saying: I should have let him drink. He lay and moaned. 'What do you want?' His eyes were wet, he tried to speak but could not. "Vo… vo…vod…" "Vodka?" I asked. He was as happy as a child. He blinked furiously: that's right, I do. And I said to him mockingly: "Here you go, drink," and gave him the finger. "He wants vodka! You drank a lot of my blood along with this vodka. It broke you, so now you can lie there, and everything will go my way. You tormented me so much, you ruined my life!" He lay there, his eyes closed, and he pressed my hand. He pressed it tenderly, like in the beginning, when our love started. On one of those days an angel certainly pushed me, and I found an exercise book of his, Seryozha. I started to move the furniture, for some reason, and found it behind the cupboard. It was a thick exercise book, and the pages were yellow, it was old. Between the pages there were a few photos – a childhood photo with his mother, as a student, with me, at the factory, with his daughter, at the factory again. He wrote out all the songs that he heard, ones that the people sing, or by the singer – Pugacheva, Leshchenko, and Cuban songs, and he also wrote his own. The last pages were messy, you couldn't make them out, about love: "Dear… forgive me… The bright sun of a sinful life…" When he did write this? A year before? Four years before? Did he scrawl it when he was drunk and forgot about it? I suddenly burst into tears, I ran to him and cried: "Couldn't you tell me in words?" and I tore up the entire book, imagine, all the pages. And I tore up the photographs. And he just looked, silently, his mouth started to open. Don't you remember how he could smile? He smiled so gently, and you could forgive him everything. But here he forgave me. I also nagged him that he worked at the factory for nothing, was wrong to be direct and honest, perhaps he should have bargained, or had a career, made the right friends, and we wouldn't have ended up poor. He drank in the last years because life flew by, and we flew by with it. You make sure, Seryozha, that you don't act foolishly, like Uncle Kolya did: be able to pretend, make the right friends... And teach your son: the main thing is not to become a worker. We didn't really understand much, we were stupid, trusting, country bumpkins..."

"What? You shouldn't talk like that!" I looked straight at her, blinded by memories.

Protest On The Run

After I had written three books and won two prizes, I founded my own movement and began to protest on the streets.

I protested "for free will, for a better lot". Protesting was always like a wind for me. A wind, because wind is particularly strong when you are running. And when I protested, I always ran – when attacking, and when retreating.

This is something comical about a runner, but running gives you an advantage. Running is a sensitive activity.

Time photographs us, but we do not need to stay still. The more swiftly we run, the more generously we are showered with flashes.

Frequently, when I remember my revolutionary running, I think that this running was always devoted to my girlishly tender and matronly coarse other half at the time, Anya. I was running away from her and towards her.

I went to Voronezh to stir up a protest. She felt coldly about my departure. Indifference disguised offense – I gave little attention to her, distracted by a single multitude of other people. She was sensitive and vulnerable, but restricted herself to harsh words and an empty expression in her eyes.

The autumn was cold that year. I was in charge of boys and girls, and the organization that was named "Hooray!" in honor of my book. Yes, with an exclamation mark. Uncle Kolya Bolbas gave his approval over the phone.

I took my faithful comrade Artyom, a first-year philosophy student, to Voronezh. There was an officer and old woman in our train compartment. The old woman curled up on the top bunk. We drank with the officer.

"I saw shadows crawling past, I was on watch, I fired at the shadows, everyone came running out, screaming, shooting, shooting... A battle started. It turned out they were Czechs. I ran, and in the darkness – bang – I ran right into one of my brothers. We fell down and both screamed. That's what war is like, boys – a lot of running around!"

Artyom listened delightedly. I listened with half a smile and thought: tomorrow we will have our own war. Our running.

And then it was tomorrow. All day I travelled around Voronezh, preparing the evening demonstration. There were no roads in the city, no work, and a lot of grey walls with obscene graffiti – on the topics of sex and politics.

Dusk fell early, bluish-black. We gathered at an intersection, to march to the city center and hold a rally. A banned rally. The piercing wind blew chaotically. The evil wind was everywhere, it got into your bones and gnawed them, sucking out the contents. I pressed the heap of flags, red and yellow, to my body, as if hoping to warm myself with them. Then I handed out these flags in the crowd – red and yellow. Artyom handed out fireworks: you pulled a string and a flame would fly out.

We were left to our own devices, 200 young people, from Voronezh, Verkhnaya Khava, and Anna (there is a town called Anna in the Voronezh Region). We marched. I was in front, in a short blue coat, a bright strap across my shoulder that was connected to a light, white megaphone.

I pressed the button and heard my shout, as if it came from someone else. The shout went behind me and was carried far away by the wind.

We walked faster and faster – into the wind.

I felt like a sail, taut and rough, my skin became part of my clothes, and the wind pushed my cry back into my throat. Hissing and a flare: Artyom lit the first firework, and everyone ran, illuminated by the fires on the run. The wind could not cope with the fire bought from a shop. Hissing and flares. Hissing and flares., We were photographed by the Russian revolution itself, and it buried our crazy, young faces in its inexhaustible card index.

We flew out from the corner and ahead of us, they were waiting on the square, standing in a line, shaken by the wind….

We rushed towards them and stopped. They were led by a police general – a heavy-jowled samovar. We were led by me – a skinny guy with a megaphone.

"You're not going to Moscow today!" With a boss's hand he tore a burning firework from someone and shoved it in my face. I moved back.

"Freak!" I heard someone cry, and Artyom spat in his face.

Grey chains, suddenly forming a wedge, ran into us, cowering in response. And a fight began – a hot lump in the wind, with a scrape of heels, blows, yelling and screeching. In the heat of this collective declaration of hatred, I was taken away from there, from Lenin Square. A strong arm grabbed by neck from behind, like a python, and suddenly it turned out that the four people around me were not my friends, but enemies in civilian clothing.

Beatings in the car, beatings on the way, beatings at the interrogation.

During a break, I was taken to a separate room which stank horribly of something sour and rotting, and I was photographed.

"Turn around!" the cop said. And I turned in profile. "Don't twitch!" My cheek twitched, expecting a blow.

At night I was taken away with a gun in my back under the black sky. And it was impossible to flee from there, from the torture fortress of the Black Earth. The sky was black, stretched out, without any stars.

Although why was I worried? Some lowlife really was tortured that night (the louder he shouted, the harder he was hit) until he passed out, but what about me? I was hit in the throat, in the sides, a fist hit my cigarette out of my mouth... (Most of our comrades, by the way, including Artyom, were able to get away that evening, without being caught). And so I turned on the irony: "circle of hell" or "circles" – this is what I called the holes in the iron doors of the cell. Filled with blinding electric light, they drilled through my brain with greetings from the outside, as if a little bird was about to fly out of each hole, and there would be whole flock of them.... The birds would chirp, flying about our dark cell, hitting the stone walls!

I was motionless, squashed in the dark by the bodies of criminals arrested for hold-ups, I felt stupefied, beaten, and I couldn't close my eyes, hypnotized by the glare of those little round holes. I kept waiting for birds, at least one. The circles mocked me. I passed my hand over my neck, feeling the bruise. They even took my cross away before putting me in the cell, the heathens! Probably so I didn't slit open my veins with the cross....

When I was released and inundated with calls and text messages, I was very upset: Anya was silent. I called her. She spoke feebly and indifferently, evidently watching television in her dressing gown. She didn't know about anything that had happened. She wasn't interested in me, she didn't search for my name on the Internet, and she didn't give a damn how the expedition to another city had gone.

I was held in a cell for over 24 hours – she didn't know. When I told her, she drawled: "Right, I see," at the other end of the line she shrugged her shoulders, which were warm after a bath.

And then there was Moscow in the winter, where I also ran, avoiding snowdrifts and slipping. My home was searched. I ran into the police in my entranceway. The two cops looked at each other, and I ran away. I hit my knee on dirty ice – it left a black mark on my jeans.

On that day a whole division swarmed into my apartment, scaring Anya, who was much more tender toward me than before, and pregnant with our child Vanya. They set up an ambush, but she managed to call me. Poor Anya, she was terrified by this attack: she wanted comfort. But they also chased me through Moscow. The activist Stepan, who wore glasses and had steel teeth, and was a football fan, was caught by his house, where I was hiding, and he helped me to run out through the back entrance. We ran away, the snowstorm whirled around us, and behind us there were shouts. We vanished in the snow.

A wanted man, in the evening I brazenly went into the center to the birthday party of a friend, a successful journalist: hardcore officialdom was gathered there, and at the table everyone made fun of my misadventures. Someone even joked: "You just keep running!" As I left the party, I was taken in. I crossed the boulevard on the corner of Petrovka Street, and a lanky man hit me. A second later I came to by the statue of the crucified Vysotsky, and from all sides men came running. Dark cars stopped and men jumped out. A bus with OMON troops, rumbling loudly, drove on to the pavement, and stopped by Vysotsky. I smiled in the clouds of snow, and the operative camera shone with the round light of a spotlight. Flashes. First one, then another. Here everything came to an end.

Games of hide and seek. I was chased, caught, tagged, and then they sent me away, happy…. But after two years elections came. First there was the sweetness of an Indian summer, photographs for posters, which would be hung all over the country. But nothing came of it. The portraits were not used. An ultimatum, a supreme cabinet, the lock clicked. It was all the way thing happened in vulgar and garish films. I got out into the corridor, tricked the guards and ran away. I remember running down the stairs: clump-clump-clump! I ran deliriously, blindly, as if I were flying, and my heart was thumping wildly.

I passed my tongue over my lips. Pink foam. I had run too much. Oh, this trace of your lipstick, my dear.

Oh revolution, my left-wing girlfriend! I gave a lot of my young energy to our illegal running, cheating on measured movements.

For I also had Anechka, my home, supper, children's laughter, the dressing gown and the family album.

And perhaps whatever I did, life would be running in a circle, and tomorrow I would go out on to the square once more?

The Adventures Of The Rabble

No, I want to talk about it in more detail. In more detail, I say. About how I tried to get into Parliament and was stopped half a step from it.

I was given security guards, because I got into the final stage of elections. Trained guards and mirror-glass cars with tinted glass – so no one killed me.

But I immediately wanted the guards to believe in me, if only a little. They should be surprised that I wasn't like the people they used to drive and protect. I was skinny and modest. And I wore a poor man's sweater, lilac, old, which my father used to wear.

Through the sun of the Indian summer our black, mirror-glass car drove. My cell phone rang.

"Yes?"

"Sergey Alexandrovich? My name is Mila. My surname is Smirnova. I want to congratulate you. You're a big success. A deputy and a writer. And you're so young, as well! In the first three! On the ballots all over the country," she had the voice of an energetic smoker. "I represent a publishing house." She named it. "We heard that you have a book ready. Is that right?"

"A manuscript".

"You're terribly busy at the moment. But it would be wonderful! We'd like to be friends with you!"

"I suggest we meet in two hours. There's a Coffee House by Mayakovskaya."

"Thank you! You're also a clairvoyant. Our windows look out on it. See you soon!"

"Sixth, sixth," the security guard with a white wire in his sticking-out ear mumbled. And something I didn't catch.

This was the third day they'd been driving me around. They had impenetrable faces and used few words.

I thought that I was behaving simply, easily with them.

I wanted to win their hearts with kindness. The driver was a beer drinker, and the security guard was a real vodka drinker. Hot breath broke through his narrow grey lips, from his meaty nostrils, and it seemed that he wanted to open his mouth wide, wrinkle his nose like a clown and howl wildly. How much tension and humiliation had they already experienced, covering someone with their own skins!

"Who are you talking to?" I asked on the first day.

"Didn't you notice anything?" the guard even thrust out his chest. "That's our escort!"

I saw the escort out of the corner of my eye. It hung back behind us, and as we approached our destination it moved ahead and went to investigate whether there was any threat, and reported the situation to the guard's wire. When we arrived, they were already waiting for us, a gang of four, who had all got out, the doors of their car were all open.

But only two were close by. The driver Tolya and the security guard Kolya.

On the first day, on Bolshaya Dmitrovka Street, clogged with cars and people, I recognized my former love, the poetess Polina, her black dress and leather jacket.

I wound down the dark glass:

"Hey!"

I moved over and made room for her.

"Would you like a lift?"

She climbed in. She didn't show that she was surprised. Just like those other two.

"To the intersection." She shook her luxuriant hair.

A mass of darkness, richly crimson at the ends. Eight years ago I loved her and her hair madly.

Like in the old days, she smelled of childish French perfume (I forget the brand, and asked her. She sang the name, happy every time, but I forgot again). She exuded a peaceful, still fair weather cold, the autumn was stuck in her hair and in the folds of her leather jacket.

"Did you hear about my affairs?"

"I don't envy you."

"How are yours?"

"How are my what?"

"Your affairs?" I said with a challenge.

"Utterly dismal. Oh," she said to the driver, "Could you stop here?" And added: "Thank you so much."

She slammed the door. She disappeared into the crowd. Why did I need this meeting?"

"Despair" – what a word! She once plunged me into despair, slamming a door.

"Utterly dismal," I sighed, and added in apology: "I was in love with her. She was just a girl. Now she's put on weight. And become darker."

They were both silent. I felt that my forehead and cheekbones were turning red, as if I had bent over a hot samovar to see my reflection in the wet copper. Had I ever loved her? Ever loved her truly? Had I loved myself? It would be great to jump out of the car at this moment, to abandon everything, to disappear from this glorious, sickening life, to catch up with her, to return to that time as a teenager, when I was free!

"Sergey, go back to your place, please," Kolya mumbled, without turning around.

"Is that important?" I crawled back, behind him.

"They kill the person in the driver's place."

Tolya was driving, and oblivious to us.

He had the manners of a robot, but on the second evening of our strange union, Kolya made a blunder. We walked in, and got into the elevator. The elevator as if thought for a while, then screeched upwards, and something made a noise above us. Something was lying on the roof of the elevator. Kolya raised his eyes to the flashing ceiling, which he could reach with his bare head, and misery ran across all the muscular lines of his face.

He put his hand on the holster on his hip and began to stroke it.

"What's wrong?" I asked.

The nightmare of his blue eyes replied to me. He wasn't looking at me, he was looking upwards. Some hooligan had probably broken down the door to the elevator shaft and thrown a garbage can out. The fragments and left overs were rising together with us.

"Nikolai," I called him, and with my finger I touched his bulky body, jabbing my finger lightly into his stomach.

In the guard's eyes, I could read a taut misery: a bomb was going to blow up, and we'd plunge to the bottom, a bunch of bloody flesh and fragments.

We went out on to the landing. He smacked himself in the forehead. His grey lips came to life, reddening:

"Sorry, I was lost in thoughts."

So, this was the third day of being with these men, and for the third day the Indian summer was continuing, and the publisher called.

At midday I arrived at Coffee House at Mayakovskaya.

A triangular face, pale with powder. A coarsely knit green sweater. Narrow glasses. Yellow hair cut short. A puffy mouth. Her voice didn't deceive me, she smoked incessantly.

I hadn't had breakfast yet, and ordered a sandwich and grapefruit juice. She ordered a long black coffee.

The guard walked outside the window, with his right profile to us, with the wire in his ear: he would pass a gaze over us now and then.

Puffy lips make you expect slow speech, but Mila unleashed a flood of words, so that her tongue jumped out on to her upper lip.

"Will you give us the new things you're working on?" She gave me her business card. "We'll take it without any discussion. We need you as a serial author. I've thought up a new niche for you: socially active realism."

"What's that?"

"It's you! Young, energetic, lucky. Handsome. Can you write for us? Write whatever you want. You'll manage. Keep a diary. We can pay you. We'll give you a decent print run."

"How much?"

"A big one. We'll pay you like for a bestseller. You won't come off badly!"

"I'm not a serial writer," I said, biting into the sandwich. "I'm not prepared to violate paper according to schedule."

"That's a shame. You should start to write blindly. Off the top of your head. People will say hooray. You like the word 'hooray', don't you?"

"Alas."

"What?"

"Alas, I love the word 'hooray'".

"So that's agreed then?"

"I'll send you the new thing I'm working on, and we can meet again."

"You can't run away from me!" She shook with artificial laughter, and then choked quite genuinely. She coughed. "Shall we pay the bill? Should I pay for the writer?"

"I'll pay."

I had already forgotten about the existence of the publisher. All around, with the intimacy of a lavish garden, the "Indian summer" was heard - made itself felt, with the screeching of tires and roaring of engines. Indian summer. Babel-summer, summer-Babel, Babel-summer, I turned over in my head. A time that was short and pretentious like Babel's prose. Hospice weather. Deathbed comfort. A few days, like presents, soon they will be dropped, broken and swept away, and you breathe in the minutes. In summer you are languid and relaxed, as for the heat, so what, you yawn in the shade, but you take fragile surprises from autumn with shaking hands.

A photographer was waiting for me by the café. I had to pose for him, so my portraits would soon hang on billboards all over Moscow, and all over Russia. He was young, tall and shy.

"Let's go in, we'll drink some tea," I said.

"Thanks, I'm full," he said in a broken voice. "Please stand here."

The guard studied the photograph with furious attention.

"Opposite the Coffee House?" I asked. "You'll get an ad for the café."

"No, they'll put another background on the photo," the youth stuttered a little.

I stood opposite the front window with a picture of a cup and coffee beans. The sun was in my eyes.

"Don't frown, please. Open your eyes."

I felt that everything was going to end badly. Someone lightly blew in my ear and whispered, ticklishly: Seryozha, you're a sun agent. While the days are bright, your victory road is running. But with the frosts – another ear heard – expect a disaster. And when the first snow falls, you'll just rest for good – both ears rang out with joy, and I blocked them.

The guy clicked without stopping. As soon as he started taking pictures, he stopped stuttering, and gave me orders:

"A step forward... Shoulder to the right... Raise your hand... In a fist... Now your palm towards me... And lift your head up..."

I wouldn't have trusted these distractions, maybe it was just my imagination running wild, if at the same time I hadn't received news from people. I had angered the very top. I jumped into the mire of politics and crossed it with fantastic strides. I ended up on the forbidden asphalt strip. In front of me were forty meters or so (by the number of days) to the finish line, to a new level of battle and fate. So far I was jumping on mounds, the jumps missed. They yawned, disdainfully assessing the age of the jumper. And the system became furious, now that it had discovered something alien. On his own. Unacceptable.

"Smile... Don't look at me, look to the side... Say something... Open your mouth wider..."

The sunny day was replaced with a sunny day. I met a colleague. He was also a candidate. A banker.

He was already waiting in a practically empty, tinted restaurant among the squinting light. He was old enough to be my father, and doomed to become a deputy, but I was higher than him on the list. He stood up, he was short. With a hill of a mouth and a slope of a nose.

I shook his hand. I had never seen him before. He had a gold watch on his wrist, super-duper, while the sleeve of my sweater was torn, I had just noticed. And he also seemed to notice:

"Don't you want to change clothes?" he asked a little disdainfully. "Or is that the fashion these days?

"The banker's hand was pressing mine hard, and I firmly resolved to also call him the familiar form of the second person.

"Fashion for the people? Have you been sitting here long?"

"No," he said. "I ordered sturgeon cutlets."

"Order a soup," I said. "Do you like shark soup?"

"It's very fatty..."

"It's thick. Cancel the order! Don't mix fish with fish!" And I shouted to the waitress. "Down with sturgeon! We don't want cutlets! Two shark soups for us!"

Like shouts at a protest. The banker shuddered in his silvery suit.

I stirred the black jelly, put the spoon in my mouth and licked it blissfully. And I was pleased to see the man opposite me frowning, turning dark. He began to fill with dark as he slurped. He felt sick. In the dim room, this was especially amusing – to watch him slurping and becoming gloomy. He wanted cutlets, golden like the day outside.... Bad luck! Have this slop instead!

"Can we talk now?" he asked,
"Sure."

And he began to eat the soup with unexpected speed, without chewing, swallowing and frowning. He plucked the starch napkin from off his lap, raised it to his face and began to rub. I felt a cheerful power. Tomorrow, perhaps, I would be destroyed, but today my knee was pressing on this bald patch. How was he. He was lower, lower, lower in the magic pyramid of power. And the sweater I was wearing was not torn, to sit in at home and cough, it was a sacred garment, imbued with smoke and the muttering of priests. Hearing the stifled voice opposite me with half an ear, I fathomed the music of secrets. The secrets roared in my head and shook. And the voice said into my ear:

"It's time to share the posts. You've got a good chance at being a vice speaker. I'd like to be the head of the committee... for industry... Only Tsygankov is against it. Do you know Tsygankov? But if you support me, he won't be a rival... And in exchange..."

I raised an eyebrow and remembered the first day of this "Indian summer": and why did I meet my ex-girlfriend then? Was it so that I would remember: there are people for whom any external success is zero.

"Accepted," I said. "I hope I can sort this out."

"Really?"

"Horrible soup," I pushed aside the full bowl and gave a meaningful look at his empty bowl. "I don't like shark anymore. It's real shit! Eh?" He grunted.

"I won't bother you anymore." And I added mockingly: "Lexeich".

"What?"

"You're Lexeich. That's your patronymic. I'll pay. Ciao, mate! I've got another meeting here."

I kept my head straight while he shook my hand, stood up and walked around me. I noticed out of the corner of my eye: in the corner a shadow rose and slipped away – his bodyguard.

I held my head as if kettle drums were booming the whole time. But in my eyes, there was the alien and mad ring: "Shh – shh – you're flying…"

I moved my chair back with a scrape. The bodyguard Nikolai looked attentively, his blue eyes shone in the semi-darkness. I was plunged into an anticipation of despair. What would it be like, this bottom, which was despair? In what form would despair come? And this angel Kolya – was he perhaps my murderer? It was uncertain who was in command of him? These men were obviously shadowing me. It was easier to control me under their convoy. But also easier to beat me up.

At night they drove me to the dacha, where my young son was staying. We drove along a country road. The road wound and was covered in rocks, it was dark and empty, and I forced myself to relax, I lounged on the back seat, prepared for the possibility that we were going to stop. Kolya, opening the door in anticipation, would drag me out on to the side of the road, push me into the forest, and aim the barrel at me….

I fell asleep, and had delirious dreams. I woke up, and the car had stopped.

"What's going on?"

"We've arrived," Kolya said gruffly, opening the door for me.

And a few hours later, it was an early, sunny morning. They took me and drove me back to the city.

"Nikolai, you look a lot like my uncle. Although he's dead. He's from Orsk," I said. "And had the same name as you?"

"How's your son?" Kolya asked, turning around for the first time.

"He's ill."

"What's wrong with him?"

"He has a cough."

"My daughter had an operation today," Tolya said. "Appendicitis. She screamed with pain at night. Everything's fine now. She's lying in bed and resting."

"You didn't get any sleep at all, I suppose?"

"We don't sleep at all anyway," he snorted. "We've been together for a year now. Nikolai takes the first metro train. He commutes from Medvedkovo. I'm closer, I come from Otradny. We gather in the center. Half an hour, and off we go."

We returned to Moscow, the north wind was blowing. And suddenly they were demanding for me to capitulate. I came to the office where a secret aide was waiting – a high-flying clerk in a brown tweed jacket. He was flying higher than me. He had wild, overgrown black southern eyebrows and a moustache of the same kind.

When I entered the office, I found myself face to face with him. With one arm, he embraced me and pulled me, and with the other he turned the key.

He said that I had taken a lottery ticket, but that now it had to be returned, because this was a decision of the head of state:

"It's in the interests of the state for you not to be here."

"The state has some strange interests…"

"Do everything as I say. Or otherwise, you'll simply go back to being," he searched for the words, and pronounced them harshly: "one of the rabble".

He moved to the attack. Money, we'll give them money. A position. Or you'll fall in the mud. It could be jail. And everyone will turn away from you. It could be a brick. A brick will fall on you.

"We'll go to the electoral commission, you'll sign a paper. We don't need a scandal."

Behind me there were blinds. I could hear Moscow with the back of my head: the piercing laughter of girls, old people mumbling, someone honking a horn. And catching support from the outside noise, I thought: there, beyond the blinds, there are unusual, brave people. They are few, but they do exist. It's quite elementary – to obey a man with bushy eyebrows and a moustache, he's stronger, but the others, furious, lonely and powerless – can I betray them? Why should I obey – to cross myself out, as if I had done something wrong?

"No."

"So, no... You're not getting out of here, you got it?"
And I deceived him.

I made out that I agreed to everything and wanted to have a cup of tea. He said that the tea would be brought to me, and I told him I wanted to be alone for five minutes, just five minutes, in the next room. A minute was enough to tell the guard who was sitting motionless in the corridor: "I'm going to the bathroom, I'll be back", to rush to the stairs, run downstairs, tell the driver who came hulking towards me: "I'm going to get cigarettes", and while he thought about this, to throw my body around the corner.

On Tverskaya, there were taxi drivers hanging about by their beat-up cars.

"Five hundred," one driver said.

I nodded.

He drove me quickly.

I ran into the entrance way, and my telephone started going off. I went into the elevator, there was a rustling noise again, but not so loud, evidently the garbage on the roof had decayed and become lighter. The guard droned: "Where are you? They're looking for you here. I'm giving my phone..." the elevator crawled through the rustle of garbage, and I hung up.

For two days, I lived behind an iron door. I took a bath over and over again. I lay up to my neck in the hot water. They couldn't decide what to do. They were waiting. Outside the window, the autumn was blazing greasily, and the trains of the Kiev station were chugging back and forth. In the evening I saw how watchfully the beam of the light spread over the wheels of the dark train. Food ran out instantly, while the Internet was inexhaustible. The anger against me (five publications an hour) reached a boiling point, but did not reach its target, it only blinded me with the flat, stupid color of the monitor. My wife was at the dacha with our son, and I called her on the land line: my son was crying and coughing.

The publisher wrote me an email: "Seryozhenka! I beg you! Where's the manuscript?", so I sent it to her. Then I got a short reply. "I apologize for being rude. Let's meet. A.F." And the weather outside the windows of the building came crashing down! After staying with us for a week, the "Indian summer" was leaving.

The guys didn't ask any questions. The guard met me by the apartment, and I got into the car. We said nothing the entire journey, only sometimes he whispered into the wire. I whistled as we drove.

The clerk was wearing a narrow suit of mourning. He flung open the heavy door in silence. A demon was sitting there. A big boss. He roared, and his spit boiled. His heavy words flew about the office.

I went out and ran into the clerk, who looked at me with hope, but I shrugged my shoulders, and he grabbed his moustache, as though it were on fire. Standing next to the clerk was the short banker, and he averted his eyes.

"Hello, Lexeich," I couldn't resist saying.

"Yevgeny Alexeyevich," he said distinctly.

I went down into the café below the office. A pork chop and a mug of dark beer.

"Hello."

"Seryozhenka, my dear. Congratulations! You've written a wonderful book! Everyone here's delighted buy it. When can I see you?"

"In half an hour? By Mayakovskaya, OK?"

"OK, of course, OK!"

I had polished off half the mug when my wife called.

"He's ill. The ambulance is coming. We're going to hospital."

"Lord have mercy!"

The guard opened the door of the mirrored car for me, and sat in the front.

"Mayakovskaya," I said.

"Did you hear?" the driver ask.

"What?"

"It's on the news already. You've been removed."

He turned up the radio.

"Can you drive me to Mayakovskaya?" I asked playfully, hiding a gaping hole.

At Mayakovskaya they both got out.

"All the best," Nikolai chewed the dead air.

"Life is long. Maybe we'll meet again?" Anatoly smirked.

"Guys! Just one question. How did I appear to you? Did I cause you any stress? Was I a good person?"

"You were... and will be! At your age!" the driver chuckled.

"You're a decent person," the guard drawled. "A bit sensitive."

"Sensitive?"

"What, did you think we didn't know words like that," Tolya shook. "We're not serfs."

"But wasn't I simple? I was always on good terms with you... I wanted to be honest..."

"That's a bad thing," the guard said, and frowned severely.

We hugged. First I hugged Kolya, and he whacked me on the back. Then Tolya, more formally, with a sense of humor. The car escort was dark next to us. No one got out.

The publisher was late.

She flew to me. I could see by her face that she already knew.

"Did you jump too high? Young man, I'll have a cappuccino, orange shake, Caesar salad, a veal sandwich and Parliament Lights cigarettes!"

"Water," I asked.

"Do you realize that people spend all their lives trying to achieve this? You lost everything! Don't you feel the sort of times we are living in now?"

"What sort?"

"Did you at least get some sort of foot in the door there? Rip off something for yourself?"

"That's not important to me. I'm going to write."

"What? Leaflets on lampposts?"

"What's important?"

"Success."

She finished eating, while outside it grew darker and colder.

"Sorry, I must be off." She took out 500 rubles. Violet like the old sweater I was wearing.

"It's my treat…"

"Forget it…"

She vanished.

"Are you finished," the waiter asked.

"Wait a minute…"

I tore a piece off her unfinished sandwich. I looked at the burning cigarette butt. I added 100 rubles, pink like success, and walked out.

"Despair" – what a word! I knew nothing but despair as I ran through icy Moscow, and it gleamed. I grimaced, panting, my teeth were freezing, but I rinsed them with steam, the steam heated them a little. I ran through the underpass from one side of Tverskaya to the other, and began to flag down a car. But the cars had frozen into a sparkling snowball. I jumped up and down with my arm outstretched. Shoes, summer shoes, clomped in this dance. The thin sound could not be heard through the traffic jam – in the general beeping and monotonous hooting. The criminal hooting sound grew along with the quacking. I jumped out, clutching the post, and a black car flew past. Illuminated by bright turquoise happiness, with its right wheels it hit the pavement. A car with a hot piece of power. It was me driving past myself.

It washed over me with a flash and drove on with a momentary photo of my defeat.

I pulled my hand away from the column. I ran.

I ran, falling, becoming entangled with the passers-by, sometimes flailing my arms out at the cars, and then ran again.

There was blackness over the city. Blackness above the wires and their flashes. The lights, with their cunning light, separated the grey from the black – grey smoke floated under the blackness, the grey car smoke went billowing. These lights themselves, multi-colored flashes, scarlet and gold, seemed accidental. The essence, the real appearance of the world, was this – black and grey. And weightless ash went flying – the predecessor of a snowfall....

This was not a city with a decorous center, but a hollow bowl. And I was running along the bottom of this hollow bowl.

And there was MacDonald's. Through the warm restaurant I walked to the free bathroom. Tapping. Numb feet in summer shoes. "Let me take your order!" came a shout to the right. To the left there were chewing noises. From the tiles, puddles smiled broadly.

They smiled: "Now you're the rabble".

Afterwards

When I got home, I could hardly find the willpower to open the window, make the bed and get undressed.

I was thirsty, but powerlessness won, and I didn't move. Outside the blinds, a train shunted along sleepily, and the pillow blended with my cheek into an airy pulsating fabric. My pulse was quiet, soon I felt a drop. I spun around, I writhed about, I turned into bubbles, which furiously and musically rose upwards. By the plastic neck we burst and disappeared. My dream didn't end, and once more, there was prickly flight along transparent walls, again the coarse blue neck flashed by, but we fled once more, burst once more, and firm and light, we hurried upwards.

I woke up. My mouth was completely dry. Feeling around, I took my cell phone from the table, which showed me that it was 1 p.m. The eternal train was chugging past the building. How long had I been asleep?

For some reason, holding the cell phone in my right hand, by old habit, I crawled to the kitchen, with my left hand I raised the dumbbell of the kettle, poured a rough stream through my teeth, went back to the room, opened one blind, and left the other one sleeping, and looked into the murky window of the telephone. I threw it down, and with a dull thud it fell on the papers on the table, and I started dressing groggily. Clumsily dancing in my pants leg, with a T-shirt half over my head, I looked at this table. In the half-light, the papers were like shadows of papers. "Baper," I said as a child instead of paper. I talked like this for a long time. Baper. Bapers, a huge amount of them, covered the table. Bold proclamations, which were scary to read again now, and their bold style was a nasty joke. Important projects that had to be torn up. An unneeded newspaper with my photograph. Business cards, a pile of them, squares with names and numbers. And there was the red-skinned, shiny exercise book. I started to keep a diary in it on the advice of the publisher, and had covered two pages with messy handwriting. Now I looked at it with disgust. To peel off the moist red cover, and there were flying letters. To read it, to force myself to read it to the last phrase, frozen over the void, and run. To the bathroom, of course. To drown in warm water.

The telephone was silent. Outside the window there was a new episode of a nature film. In black and white.

And then I remembered everything. Unexpectedly I remembered. I thought about nature, and the last chapter suddenly came to life in a second. My child was in the hospital. Yes! My son! And immediately, forgetting about my hostility towards the table, I lunged at it, pulled the telephone out of the papers and called my wife.

"Hi."

"I'm listening! What do you want?" the thin sound multiplied in her voice with a set of razors.

"How is he?"

"How could he be? Do you want to help or chat?"

"How is he? Better?"

"Not good."

"Does he have a temperature?"

"It's lower in the morning. They're giving him antibiotics."

"Is the hospital OK?"

"It's awful. If you were a deputy we'd move to another one."

"Why are you talking about that... Obviously I never will."

"Really? When are the elections? How much longer do you have to wait?"

"Oh... Wait. Don't you know?"

"What is it then?"

"Well... yesterday... Don't you have a radio? Didn't anyone tell you?"

"What?"

"Well... yesterday..." guiltily I searched for the words, and said: "Basically, I was removed. From those damned elections. Darling, hey! Take pity on me."

There was a thud at the other end.

"What do you mean?" she drawled. "Pity you? Are you joking? How can that be – you were removed?"

"I'm not joking."

"What for?"

"Well... You know... I'm dangerous for them. I criticized them."

"Why did you do that?"

"What was I supposed to do, praise them?"

"Damn you," she said matter-of-factly and hung up.

Just the same as always! I even doubted whether she understood that I had been defeated.

We had lived together for five years now – our son was one year old.

His illness distracted me from thoughts about the defeat.

I had to go to him, I realized. To the Moscow Region. To my son. To see him, to hug him, to appear to him – that was important. I would take a suburban train, travel to Pushkino, and there on the platform I would ask where the hospital was. I wouldn't call Anya just yet, I decided, she'd calm down. She'd become gentle by the time I arrived, and even start to regret her anger. That was what I was dreaming of when the cell phone I had put in my pocket started to ring. The first call of the day.

"Dima. Ryazan" was reflected in the mirror.

"Hello Ryazan!" I barked cheerfully, out of habit

"Hi there. We've come to Moscow. We'd like to see you," the voice droned gloomily.

"Write down my address..."

I went outside, it was icy and cold. We met at a beer bar by my building, which was playing deafening cheerful pop music. There were eight of them. In black leather jackets. Dima was their leader. He had a black mane of hair, he was skinny, and an old scar of a wrinkle on his forehead.

"We came to find out what to do next."

"I don't know, to be quite honest."

I bought each of them a mug of draught beer. I raised the glass and saw the world as being golden and kingly.

"I don't know, brothers," I repeated.

"Who shall we go after?" An unknown to me teenager with shaven temples asked.

"That's the past," I snorted.

"We got up early, when it was still dark, and we came to you.... we came here..." said Dima, studying me with a glowering look. He had the habit of repeating words. "Where shall we go? We're ready. With you we're... we're ready... we were a gang. We're a gang... we'll throw rocks, let them tie us up. If you want we'll go to Red Square – we'll follow you... shall we go?"

"Don't do it, guys," I whispered through the foam.

I'm the rabble, with an angry wife and a sick son. But a guy came along who didn't betray me, and brought other guys to Moscow. Isn't that enough? But where's Voronezh? Voronezh is silent."

"Thanks, guys. I have a simple mission for you: return to Ryazan. Forget about me. I only want one thing: everyone who followed me should find a place. No one should suffer because of me."

"Shall I punch you?" a balding guy in round glasses jumped up. "You offered us sin! And this is a leader..." He waved his arms foolishly, like a skier.

"Sit down, Kostya. Are you nuts?" Dima pulled him hard and he fell back down, he quickly calmed himself down with a big gulp, splashing his glasses, and he blinked behind them.

We finished off the beer. I went over to the bar, paid and left, saying goodbye with a nod of my head. Out of pity, so they didn't hope for miracles, and so they got things straight: I wasn't their leader anymore. They nodded – eight of them, at the same time. What use was their pointless revenge? They should get themselves out of it, and the sooner the better. I went away, and in my heart there was a jubilant squeak: "Thank you, guys!"

I decided to go straight to the train station, without going home first, and to the hospital from there. The metro was next to the building. The building, which had thick walls and was from the Stalin era, stood surrounded by railway lines in front of it and student dormitories behind it. Here was the inside of Kutuzovsky Prospekt. The lines stunk of tar, and the dormitory of some brew. Both of the stenches had a similar rankness in common, which was unpleasant, mixed with cold. I went out of the beer and bar and fell into the bustle of people. Yellow faces swam past me, their eyes flashed – the dormitory inhabitants were marching in a stubborn crowd. In their eyes was the misery of Asia. Did they agree to walk together? Were they Chinese or Vietnamese? Did they come together by internal clocks or by a conspiracy and walk together? They moved along, even if they were in a separate, free flow, but it was the movement of brothers. I walked with them and felt myself to be yellow-faced, slanty-eyed and stoic. Although to my left there was a Russian guy, with a mundane meaty face, but with eyes that were narrowed with a hopeless cunning look, as if he had sworn an oath of loyalty to Asia. I noticed his eye, because he looked at me, as he walked beside me. We towered above the crowd, at the same height. His face did not change its expression, but his eyes lived a smart, inquisitive life. I responded to him with a staring competition, and he turned away unwillingly. The Asians didn't look at me. They didn't push or shove. Sometimes one cried out to another. We breathed out steam, and as I breathed out the steam together with them, I felt their language. Was it Chinese or Vietnamese? What difference did it make? And so we moved along in the unfriendly rough interior, blown by the wind of winter. And we went into the metro.

We got into the car, confirming that we were the majority, and began to travel towards the center. This is the army you are worthy of, I thought, swaying in drowsy indifference among the bodies.

They started yelling, competing with the noise of the train. They squashed me, and their bodies not only swayed, they vibrated, they shook under the thick clothes from the loud, screaming voices.

Kievskaya Metro Station. The Russian guy looked at me over the shoulders and heads. The one who had walked next to me. He had grey attentive eyes. "Is he a faggot?" I wondered. "He's trying to pick me up." It wasn't a threatening look, but he was rather studying me. I also started studying him. His face was quite ordinary, shaved, his chin was pitifully doubled, chubby, but pursed lips, a hooked nose, perhaps broken, and a black knitted cap. It seemed that his gaze was indifferent to the fact that I could see it. The guy once more averted his eyes unwillingly.

Smolenskaya Metro Station.

The Asians didn't get out. I saw the platform through a gap in the bodies, where a couple was milling about indecisively, an old man and woman, they didn't get in. Although it was crowded, they'd be shoved about... It was Asia here. "Metro" is an Asian word. I started looking for accomplices with my eyes, the guy in the black hat, but I didn't find one, but there were yellow, pock-marked faces tense with shouting, sunken cheeks, trembling Adam's apples – there were more than enough of them.

Alexandrovsky Garden. The last stop.

The Asians shoved their way out the door in organized fashion. I was carried with them. A flow of people coming in the opposite direction dissolved our brotherhood. We scattered, the journey in a crowd was over. I crossed over to the Biblioteka Station.

I got into another train. There weren't many people in it, and I took a seat.

I raised my head. The grey eyes were looking at me attentively.

What a bastard! Sitting opposite me, the same guy was embarrassed for a moment, then overcame the awkwardness and a shadow of a mocking smile crept across his face. He took off his knitted hat, revealed carefully cut dark hair and hunched up. He put the hat on his lap and stared at me again.

"A bodyguard!" I thought.

And then I remembered: how could he be a bodyguard?

Who needs you now – why would they send a bodyguard for you?

An ally? A silent fan? Did he recognize me and was following me sympathetically in the underground, protecting me. What nonsense. I stuck out my tongue.

"Young man, behave yourself!" a chubby woman sitting next to him said loudly.

He squirmed, confused.

"What? What's wrong?" He said, leaning over towards her.

"I'm not talking to you... To him... The guy with his tongue out..."

Ohotny Ryad Metro Station. I leapt up from the seat, and to the cries around me of "My God!" I rushed out of the car and jumped into the next one.

The last test. I walked to the end of the car and saw that the guy had got up. He walked to the end of his car, and through the windows he stared at me. We shook, looking at each other, between us there were clattering and creaking noises. Would he shoot from one car to another? Go on, shoot! It would be great. I sat down. At Lyubanka he came to me and stood over me, one hand holding the handle bar, the other clenching the ball of his hat.

"What do you want?" I asked.

My voice was drowned in the clatter.

"What do you want?" I shouted.

"Hey, what are you shouting about?" a shaggy man leaned over me, breathing cheap alcohol, with orange stubble, that looked like it had been dyed.

The accomplice kept silent.

"What's with you? I tore out teeth in the penal battalion…" the man bent over, his face swelling up, and the skin under the stubble throbbed theatrically.

"Calm down, mate," the guy said in an absent voice and shoved the man. Chistye Prudy Metro Station.

The man loudly hiccupped (as if he was pulling out a cork with his teeth) and fell out. The doors slammed shut. I saw the man swaying and putting his hands of the marble of the walls. The guy stood over me, powerful. Rhythmically swaying. He kept me under his grey gaze.

"Get better, son!" a prayer rang out in my head, and I took my mind off the specter hanging over me. I wasn't afraid of a hitman, I had already been killed in the battle, what I wanted was for my son not be ill.

Krasniye Vorota. Komsomolskaya.

I leapt up, and he deftly got out of the way. I walked on. Above the platform, on the balcony, there were two cops leaning over the railing. Below them bustling flows of people were rushing past. The clock said 15:24. Clocks in the metro are made out of sparks. Time is a spark, a fertilization. Below the sparks was a slippery mirror that sucked up trains. I shouldn't look back! With broad strides I rushed up the escalator, feeling that the back of my head was a target.

The surface at last! I let the cold into my lungs. The Yaroslavl Station, the smoke of cigarettes and pies, kitschy music from the kiosks, train indicator panels that could not be seen properly because of the daylight, soldiers with sacks were huddled over, and beggars were walking up and down importantly. Two women were racing to a train, one was groaning, and the other was clenching her teeth, and so she was faster. I entered the hall, and winked at the tramp who appeared between the doors. I bought a ticket, went out again into the cold and stared at the panel. I turned around.

We almost bumped our heads together. The guy was breathing heavily. I stopped breathing altogether.

"What do you want?" I asked, frowning.

He asked in a bored voice:

"Going to Pushkino?"

I nodded.

He put his hand in the pocket of his coat. He took out a black object.

I clutched at his face.

He jumped back, hiding the camera.

"Off you go! What are you waiting for?" he shouted. "You'll be late." He slapped his pocket, and jumped back again.

"Who sent you?" I screamed.

"It's the elections!" He shrugged. "Don't fool around."

I stood in the empty vestibule, as the train approached for Pushkino.

Moscow was moving into the distance. The clusters of bare villages, five-story buildings and huts, a long grey wall covered in teenage colored scribble. The train squealed and clanked.

I got out at the station. By the platform steps, an old woman was selling salted cucumbers and tomatoes in separate plastic bags. Two bags lay on the wooden box by her feet.

"How do I get to the hospital?"

"Straight ahead."

"Is it far?"

"Depends how fast you walk. Twenty minutes, if you're quick."

I looked at the salted vegetables closely, as if I was listening to faint music, and she caught my gaze.

"Buy them, dear, the weather's rotten, salted vegetables warm you up."

"That's the first I've heard about that," I said in surprise.

"They seal off the damp, and warm up your whole body."

I shrugged my shoulders and looked with increasing suspicion at the transparent bags with green souvenirs of the Russian winter. And I traipsed off down the road.

A grocery store. A post office. Residential buildings. Black bushes. A wandering herd. Cars drove past. There wasn't yet any snow, but it was coming invisibly. That's the way it is before the snow falls, and this isn't just because of the frosts and the covering of ice, but in the barely visible white flickering, which is everywhere. It is not steam, but the shadow of snow, its incipience, premonition, a slight mirage. The shapes of the snow drifts have already been marked out above the earth in white chalk in the grey air, but the snow itself is not there yet. I trudged and trudged, until to the right I saw a gate with a plywood sign attached to it. On the white sign, there was a picture of a bee that resembled a tiger poised to jump.

I called my wife.

She answered after about ten rings.

With silence.

"Anya!" I said.

"What! Say something! We've got an operation going on here!"

"I'm here. How can I find you?"

"Building number six." She hung up.

Operation, frustration…. Now I just had to find the building. I called out to a nurse who was running across the road with a white sign of imminent snow.

"Over there, and to the left," she replied with shivering haste. Both the sound of her voice and her gestures foretold a snowfall.

A building with dirty windows, and in the glass there were dabs of whitewash. I pressed the call button, a rotting wooden door opened, and after leaving my coat on the hook downstairs and putting on blue shoe covers, I went to the reception room on the second floor. A desk, a woman on duty with her hair in a bun, a lamp, a paper icon of St. Nicholas, a newspaper open to the crossword puzzle, where half of the squares were already blue with the veins of solutions. On the walls was the aggressive bee which looked like a tiger, as well as a hedgehog, mole and giraffe, chubby and sad. My ward was on the right.

I pushed the door open.

My son!

I walked in and saw him right away. My dear Vanechka! He was bald, his head had been shaven. His black eyes flashed. His mouth was distorted in a delighted smile. Our eyes met, cunningly, playfully and impudently. How I missed you? Did you miss me? The two of us were conspirators.

How wonderful this blood conspiracy between father and son is, when it continues deeply and warmly – with a common breath, mutual forgiveness or even the gracious concession of the father: son, be the way you want to be, you will make you happy, I only want to keep giving, and your joy is the only thing I expect from you!

A week later he was discharged. And a week after that I went to work as a caretaker. Not that I couldn't earn money any other way. It was more of a gesture.

I had been crushed. I would never be employed as a journalist. Yesterday's friends in politics would avoid me like a leper. Yesterday's friends in literature were gloating. Only my parents were unchanged.

For bravery, I sucked down half a bottle of port, and sliding along the morning glassy ice, I went to the housing office.

Surprisingly enough, the woman there understood me immediately. She chewed something while she wrote down my details, made me sign for the equipment, and assigned me an area to work in: Kievskaya Street, building 20 from the side of the courtyard.

"The trial period is one week," she said, raising her friendly eyes, and finally swallowing the mysterious lump.

The scrape from the darkness outside the window used to seem to be the real music of slavery. This scrape does not sound torturous, it is even pleasant. You turn to your side, with your cheek on the pillow, and in the early dawn darkness someone is scraping pennies out of the frost. This sound, which alarms you, starts to lull you, and returns you to the depths of sweet oblivion.

And now I had become one of them, an outsider. I was scraping in the morning darkness. The secret of the job was simple, and came down to the measured repetition of simple movements. The main thing was to push the snow with pressure, to scoop up more and get deeper.

In a week I built hundreds of excellent snow mounds, clearing the path around the building. And I learned to distinguish friends and enemies. The clear sky was my friend. Windless weather was my friend. There was the friendly white-toothed Baimurat, who battled the snow that was blocking entry into the building. He often bore his teeth in a smile, because I gave him cigarettes.

The chief enemy was the sky that sent a snowy haze down. For a week I battled the snow, the first two days the lady from the building office picked on me, and Baimurat said "You're a saboteur", but with a laugh. The remaining three days I battled for their recognition.

Working on the city street, you gradually stop thinking about the people around you, like an actor, probably, abstract from the viewers. I wasn't worried about the passers-by, I wasn't afraid of dogs (I was armed with a spade). I was only interested in the result – to destroy the snow drifts.

However, the second day I was close to the end of clearing up, there was only twenty minutes left to scrape it away. I was terribly wet, and first I unbuttoned my coat, and then I threw it on the snowy mound. The winter broke through occasionally with a wave of freezing water through the veil of heat. But with each new blow and sweep the reddish sun became increasingly summery. My hands shook, and the blisters ached. I had to get my breath back. It was a triumph of solitude. I fell to my knees, holding on to the wooden shaft, and the large metal sheet of the spade shone in my face.

I breathed on the metal covered with lines of snow, seeing my distorted reflection: a blot for a face, and straggly hair. It seemed to me that I had been imprinted on this steel sheet. My face would now always be on this spade. A photograph of solitude. A face and a spade. I would throw snow with my face. I would stop being a caretaker, but the next caretaker would stick a spade with my face on it into the snow.

A week of working at the building office was enough for me. With the money I earned, I bought dumbbells, so that the muscles that had been roused did not go to sleep, and I bought my son children's biscuits, "with holes in them", the way he liked them.

And I gained certainty that I could work as a caretaker. Then Anya and I broke up.

To Chechnya, To Chechnya!

That spring, I managed to get a job at a glossy magazine – and I was given an assignment. They promised to pay me well if I brought back photographs and an article from Chechnya, where staff employees did not want to go. But I was supposed to travel all around Chechnya. Who would show me around and where I would stay – these were my problems.

And I flew to Chechnya.

It wasn't just about money, although I really was in need of money. It was about my loneliness. Where could I live? It didn't work out with Anya. It was also difficult with my parents. But the main thing was fatalism. "Perhaps I've already lived my life," I thought easily and proudly. "And now I need to trust fate: to come under a line of machine-gun fire behind the wall of the Caucasus…" That spring I put my life at the disposal of invisible forces.

I had a friend called Alikhan. He was originally from Vedeno, lived in Moscow, and at one time he joined "Ura!". He was swarthy, with bushy eyebrows, and fiercely flared nostrils. He saw a bright sticker in the metro and came and joined us. Alikhan didn't drink or smoke, and he had the acrid and sweet smell of fresh milk from a she-wolf. I had never smelled a wolf, but for some reason I always thought that Alikhan smelled like a wolf-cub who had just turned away from a she-wolf. We stayed in contact – we called one another occasionally.

I called him and found out about Chechnya. He said that he had an uncle living in Grozny.

"Your uncle by blood?"

"No, but's he's still an uncle… A distant uncle… He'll let you stay if I ask…"

And so I flew into the unknown. "Everyone has distant uncles," I comforted myself. "I had Bolbas."

The plane landed at noon in a bare field: the mountain towered over it, and large black birds circle overhead. Alikhan's "distant uncle" Umar turned out to be 65 years old. He met me at the Ingush airport of "Magas", and we drove to Chechnya past pyramid-shaped topol trees, past the checkpoint, past the soldiers on the side of the road looking for mines. I got the feeling that Umar had decided to give me the impression of being a cultured person from the very first minute.

"Are you a journalist? That's close to what I do. I'm a Russian language and literature teacher." He had a guttural voice, a dried-out face, and grey stubbly whiskers. "I taught it all my life. Now you might say I'm on holiday".

We sat down in the dining room on the second floor of a brick house. This house, which had been destroyed, was rebuilt by Umar. The second floor was inhabited. On the first floor, construction was still underway – the walls were bear, and there were boards and concrete dust on the floor.

"You'll come to live our Chechnya," said a woman called Zainap from the stove, who looked like a black chicken. She was about ten years younger than her husband. Go for a walk, breath in the fresh air…"

"Chechnya – that's not right," Umar interrupted. "I don't like that word. Chechnya is the wrong word. It doesn't sound proud. Chechnya-shmechnya! And I don't like the sound "ch". Do you know many good words that start with "ch"?

I thought it over.

"Chernobyl," Zainap suggested.

Her husband clicked his tongue:

"Did you have to blurt that out!"

Zainap loudly clacked the spatula as she turned over a pancake in the spitting frying pan.

"Choke," Umar chose words thoughtfully, the literature teacher. "Chikatilo."

I laughed:

"Choice, church, chestnut!"

"Chewed-up chestnut," Umar chewed his lips, and in his eyes a teenage daring appeared. "Chimp, chunks!"

"Chaff," I agreed. "What word do you like?"

He became serious.

"Ichkeriya," he said gently. But Nokhch is even better. We're Nokhchi, the children of Noah. Then the English came along. The Chechens and the English are of one blood, did you know that?"

Zainap sighed heavily, perhaps over my ignorance, and suggested:

"Why don't you take a walk around Grozny."

I nodded.

"I'll drop you off in the center," said Umar. "Go and walk around wherever you want, come back on your own, and then we'll set off, is that OK?"

"You're not a Chechen," Zainap looked at me attentively, searching for something in my face. "Don't be scared. Who will bother you?"

I nodded again, obedient to fate.

Umar and I left the courtyard, got into his grey Lada, and he took me to the city. I got out.

"There you go," he gave me a scrap of paper. "Say this address, and the driver will take you back. Fifty rubles, don't pay any more."

I was left alone in Grozny. With the feeling that I had been abandoned, and with an incomprehensible feeling of calm. The camera hung around my neck, covering my solar plexus.

It was Saturday. I walked down the central street in the noisy crowd of people, only emerging from it from time to time. I started to take photos. The crowd carried me, looking, feeling and sizing me up. The city swam past me in all its magnificent chaos. The renovated facades of tall buildings, a sparkling fountain, new pavements, fir trees, and the colossal concrete foundation of a future mosque. And next to them, high-rise buildings destroyed by bombs, wild grass, a gate with a white inscription on the rust: "Mines! Careful!" a blind and mutilated administrative building with rare glass letters from the past above it, where you could guess the slogan: "Art belongs to the people", but from the first word, only "A" was left, as though a post-modernist had intentionally knocked out the unnecessary letters. I looked around and took one photo after another: enthusiastic posters masked the holes in the walls. "Ramzan, you've only been president for a year – the city has risen from the ashes, our people are delighted!" "Children's smiles are a reward for a hero". And there were black-and-white notices on posts: "Missing Person".

The people smiled. This seemed strange. I thought they'd stab me or shoot me. But everyone I encountered was happy to pose for the camera, and the passers-by asked me: "Where are you from?". When I said I was from Moscow they became even more curious. Women selling goods at the market, stubbled guys, a legless invalid in a wheelchair, girls in headscarves and with flirtatious ribbons in their hair, and of course swarthy boys – tens. Hundreds of faces were turned to me, and every one was prepared to pose for a new photo. As if they had agreed to do so. And even a group of bearded men in black. They stopped and raised their guns. I didn't have to ask them: they opened their mouths themselves. They showed a wide variety of teeth: golden crowns, strong fangs and rotten fragments.

"You're in black?" I asked.

"If you're in black, then you're one of Kadyrov's men," the fattest and most striking bearded man said grandly.

Then I went into a café, sat down in a separate booth in the wall at a rough wooden table, pulled the old white blue blind and drank a bowl of Kalmyk tea – with milk and salt. Then I continued my walk.

"Maybe we should go somewhere?" I asked a girl who posed for me with delight, and even with lust, I thought.

She said in disappointment:

A BOOK WITHOUT PHOTOGRAPHS

"I'm not allowed."

I took her photo again many times.

Then I felt like going to the bathroom. I went into the first building I found, walked along the corridor, and ahead of me there were juicy banging noises and cries of passion. It was a boxing ring divided into pieces. Ten guys naked above the waist were hitting each other in boxing gloves. They were sweaty and breathing heavily, and I aimed the camera and started shooting: some of them looked around, shook themselves and continued hitting each other. One boxer ran out to the ropes, turned around under the flash and raised his rubber fist up high. I kept walking through the building and ended up outside again.

"Where's the bathroom around here?"

"Over there, on three fools' square," said an old man in a sheepskin hat.

"Three fools?"

"There's a statue. From the Soviet times. Three soldiers. Can you take a photo of me? Take a photo and I'll tell you more." And he continued through the flash: "Three men were shot on this square. After the first war under Aslan. Three robbers. Devils. They were taken out and shot. And the whole city watched." The camera was hanging around my neck again. "There's the toilet. There's a barn to the right of the statue. Do you see it? There are bottles around it...."

"Why are there bottles?"

"What do you mean, why? We're Muslims. You have paper, we have water. Where are you from?"

"I have a son there. The other one was killed by your lot. They kidnapped him and tortured him, and didn't give the body back to us. Take a photo of me for the last time!"

He smiled broadly to the flash: he had a strong face, a keen gaze, a white beard and a sheepskin hat that resembled a mound of buckwheat.

In the dusk I hailed down a car, and as Umar had predicted, for just fifty rubles a guy in a tracksuit drove me to the outskirts – to the brick house.

There until late at night I had supper with Umar and Zainap. Meat, pancakes and brandy.

Umar pointed at the cupboard with shiny bindings:

"My books! Yesenin, Lermontov, Kuprin. My son read them. He was killed. When the first war began, we fled to Ingushetia, our children were still at school: a son and daughter, Adym and Ama. We lived in a wagon, we froze and starved, and a bomb hit our house. We came back. We started rebuilding it. And then the second Chechen war began. In February 2000, people broke into the house – wearing masks, and holding guns. They took Adym. I shouted: "Who are you?" They hit me with the gun butt twice, I fell down and they kicked me, they broke my nose and ribs. They shoved my wife to the side. They took my son away. He was twenty years old. He was an ordinary boy, he read books. What sort of rebel was he? They put him in a pit, where the Khankala aerodrome is. One guy survived and told me about it. He said they sat in the pits for days without food or water, and only heard the roar of the planes flying overhead.

"I pray for one thing," Zainap said, giving a sigh. "That they didn't torture him. That they killed him, and were done with it."

"Everyone was tortured!" her husband interrupted her. "What are you thinking?"

I said nothing.

Finally I asked cautiously:

"What about your daughter?"

"Ama works for the police," said Umar.

"She's nothing but trouble," the woman said.

"Cut it out…" Umar waved his hand.

"What's to hide? She married poorly. She had a child, and her husband abandoned her. That's a disgrace here! He's a bastard. His family said: "Your daughter's to blame for everything!" They don't even want to see the child.

She was always such a good girl. She was good around the house, and slender, with thick hair and eyes like stars. She lives in Argun with the child, and my sister, an old lady, sits with him during the day, while Amochka is doing her police work. He's a boy, called Zelimkhanchik. He's so clever and cheerful. He doesn't know about his misfortune yet. How can that be – to live in Chechnya, and your own father doesn't recognize your existence!"

"He's a fine, fine child," Umar beamed lovingly.

"Right…" Zainap went out and quickly came back with a yellowing school exercise book. "Read this! Ama wrote poems when she was still at school. She was 13 years old. "To My Brother". Read it! I'll introduce you to her!"

"Can you read it aloud?" Umar asked sternly.

I took the exercise book, and read aloud:
Brother, who's to blame that you are gone,
Filthy pigs took you away
And where can you be found now!
Why do we need this loss, it makes me cry!
Why did the war come to our house,
Why did the winter steal you?
Russia, we will take revenge
And turn you into smoke!!!

"You?" I asked. "Russia?"

"She was young. She doesn't think like that now."

"People were brutalized," Umar said. "So many were killed. They came and killed us. What for?"

"Listen," I said. "What about before the war? Excuse me, but everyone who wasn't a Chechen was killed and thrown aside…"

"They were bandits," Zainap replied. "I was also stopped and robbed on the street. The times were like that: a lot of violence."

"You were robbed. But if you'd been Russian you'd have been killed, right?" I asked.

Umar emptied his glass:

"Your Russians were the bosses here," with a broad gesture he wiped his mouth and whiskers. I was a teacher in the village. Zinyakova was the principal, she was Russian. She hounded me, she wouldn't leave me alone. We suffered so much, remember?" He said to his wife.

"I remember, I remember! We wrote letters to the part. With no result. The Russians were in charge everywhere."

"What happened to her?" I asked.

"The Russians in Grozny lived in the center," he continued, as if he hadn't heard. "In the best houses, high-rises. When Russia started the war, your lot were the first to be killed. The bombs fell, and the Chechens left the city to stay with their relatives, and the Russians stayed in the city, in the center. You Russians killed your own people..."

"What's the use of talking? No one listens to us..." Zainap got up. "Would you like to go to bed now?"

We also got up.

In my small room, I turned off the lights and got into bed.

"You're in Chechnya, you're in Chechnya!" it beat in my head, and stopped me from falling asleep.

The door squeaked. I sat up in bed. I turned on the light. Umar was swaying. He had a pistol in his hand.

"Can't you sleep?"

The pistol was pointing at my face.

"No, I can't," I said, frowning.

"Don't be scared. It's my daughter's. She's a policewoman. I'll introduce you! Well, sleep then..."

"It's like this," he said at breakfast. "I'll give you to another person for the day. Our family is coming to visit today, they'll fill the house. You spend a day with him, stay the night at his house, and return. He's called Alkhaz. He's a cop, but a good person."

We got into a car, in the center of Grozny. Umar introduced me to Alkhaz and drove away.

Alkhaz was in a police uniform and resembled a monkey, tanned with a furrowed brow, and happy wrinkles on his face. He introduced me to his policeman friend with the name of Lecha – enormous and fat, with protruding lips and nostrils.

"He's my neighbor and we work together."

"We drove through the city in a shabby Zhiguli. In the back was Lecha with a machine-gun. Alkhaz's Kalashnikov was by my feet.

Alkhaz decelerated, wound down the window and shouted at a woman walking by.

"What are you doing, eh?"

In surprise she jumped away. He started cursing her in Chechen. The girl replied confused and hysterically.

He threw out a last word, evidently an insulting one, laughed harshly and waved a threatening finger. We kept driving.

"What happened?" I asked.

"Didn't you see? She was dressed like a slut. Girls like that should be shot! If we get a signal that a woman is living improperly, we go and call on her."

"And?"

"We explain how she should live."

Later I went with them to their police station, which was riddled with bullets and resembled a military fortification. I leafed through a thick exercise book with the latest criminal cases: statements about missing relatives.

Then we went to the stadium. It was a special day: a football match between Terek and TSSKA.

"I wonder how the fans behave here," I thought out loud.

"Quietly," said the fat cop. "They came by bus. All of the windows were smashed in Ingushetia yesterday.

We arrived at the stadium one hour before the match. There was already a big crowd. It looked as if all the men in the city had come here. Men, youths and children were running towards the stadium from all sides. In groups, laughing. They broke through the barriers of the metal detectors. But each one was searched for a long time. Kadyrov's guards were everywhere, in black uniforms, clinking bolts. Finally, with lights flashing, Ramzan's cortege drove up. This was the same stadium where his father had been blown up.

The entire stadium (with 10,000 seats) was full. We sat under the central tribune. Ramzan hung over us in a brown leather jacket, he kept clutching at his head. Next to him in a blue suit his faithful ally shuffled about – the brutally smiling Delimkhanov.

At every pass, the crowd reacted as if Chechen honor were at stake. People jumped up and down and yelled.

"O-o-o-o!" an old man wailed, clenching his fist.

Terek rolled towards the rival's goal. Goal! The stadium flew into the air as if it had exploded. Ramzan jumped and waved his hands. The world drowned in the cries of newborn babies.

"Troop withdrawal," someone shouted. "Allah Akbar," was the deafening reply.

1:0. The tribune of TSSKA fans was quiet and motionless. They weren't fans, but mannequins. Chechens poured out on to the street. They went jumping along, singing, hugging, clapping, and on their faces was a kind of physiological pleasure, as if each one of them had given birth to this ball.

A little boy, shrieking desperately, jumped on my back, and – what else could I do – I carried him halfway down the street. The two laughing cops, Alkhaz and Lecha, moved quickly alongside me.

Then we drove to Bamut – to look at a place which had once been very lively.

The village that had once been encircled and erased from the face of the Earth was green with the wild grass of early autumn. The grass rustled among the stone fragments. Opposite there was a large cemetery. Instead of gravestones, there were metal flasks. They chimed easily and melodically. There were many nameless graves with iron flasks. That was the way that martyrs were buried.

We then drove further, and by Gudermes we went

out on to the field. There was also a field there, there were no traces of any dwellings. Taking a step to the side, I discovered a small grey stone with the dark names of Russian soldiers who lay buried here. In the winter, during the second Chechen war. In the snows of a ravine. "Eternal glory!" read the inscription. The sun shone, there was a smell of damp earth, the warm, merciful wind blew around us, and the half-erased names turned dark. "Nikolayenko", "Morozov", "Yermakov" – I saw three names and remembered them.

I drank with the cops in the evening at their home in Grozny. They lived on the same floor in a five-story building, damaged and burnt-out, which several shells had hit. There was no heating. Instead, Alkhaz had installed a miraculous glass device attached to the stove: a fire burned inside it. The device heated the apartment a little. Alkhaz also had a house in the country, where his wife and three children lived. He said that once people in masks had taken his brother away in Grozny. I understood that this was a typical story. Lecha lived with his wife and three children in this mutilated building.

"When the first war began, we all fought," said Alkhaz, growing drunk. "Tanks crawled through the streets, and we set fire to them. Who fights like this – tanks on narrow streets…. We communicated by radar: brother, wait, don't set fire to that tank, it's mine. We really hunted!"

"We were hunted," I said gloomily.

"Why you?"

"Because Russians were hunted."

"There weren't just Russians there," Lecha said. "There were Chuvash. The Ossetian OMON entered the village. They tortured my uncle."

"Your uncle?"

"A distant uncle…"

While we drank vodka in the kitchen, Lecha's son appeared next to him, a two-year-old ginger boy. He took a teaspoon from the table and waved it around amusingly.

"Put it back," his enormous father said.

The child raised his eyes, saw his father's gaze and obeyed with fear.

I pointed the camera at him and clicked.

"Come here, I'll show you how you came out!"

"Come here and drink vodka," Lecha interjected.

The boy came up to him, his father grabbed him with his enormous hand, put his fluffy head against his broad knee and stuck the bottle in his mouth.

The child grimaced, made a crying noise and waved his head.

"What are you doing!" I said.

Lecha gave me a disdainful look:

"He should get used to it!"

"That's right, he should be a man!" Alkhaz beamed.

The next morning he gave me back to Umar, and drove me to his brick cottage.

Their relatives had already left, but Ama, the daughter of Umar and Zainap, was still there. It was her day off.

Ama turned out to be swarthy and long-haired, with a puffy mouth, round hips and large breasts.

She looked at me with such bashfulness and playfulness that I couldn't help suspecting that she had been prepared for me as a wife.

"Amochka suggests going to the mountains," Zainap said in an apologetic tone.

"To the mountains," I livened up. "I need to go everywhere."

"There's a wizard there," Umar said ironically. "I'm a person of the old school. I couldn't care less about all that devilry. It upsets me that we have all this heresy forced on us! You talk to her," he indicated his daughter with a nod of his chin. "She forgot about books. She forgot about writers, and doesn't know anything about scholars. She believes all kinds of nonsense."

"He's not a wizard, he's a healer," Ama said cheerfully. "Dad, you should go and see him…"

"Right… I'll go straight to him…"

"He laid his hands on me, and it was as if he turned over my insides. He guessed everything that was painful. He even said where I had a birthmark on my back. He's a clairvoyant, he knows the future."

Zainap sighed with hope.

"No, I'm not going with you," said Umar. "It's right in the south. There's nothing but forests and those.... Partisans everywhere. Anything could happen. You shouldn't go there again either, my daughter. You're a policewoman. Seryozha will be kidnapped. Who will pay for you, Seryozha," he asked without laughing, in irritation. "Or they could just shoot you on the spot."

But half an hour later we were already in a taxi, the mother, daughter and I.

We had to drive across Chechnya, to the mountain village of Makhkety.

By lunchtime we were on a broken mountain road, with a thick fir forest towering above it. My ears popped, the road was empty, the forest was green, impenetrable and endless. But on one of the turns we went up a path covered with small stones, and entered a village. The car stopped, and the taxi driver stayed behind to wait. In single file, on the edge of a rough, impassable road with deep puddles, we walked to a house – large, bright and planked. By the house there were chickens scurrying about, and a crowd of women, old and fat, with sagging, flabby faces.

"Let us through, please," said Zainap. "This is a guest from Moscow."

They did not object, and moved out of the way indifferently.

But we had to wait inside the house, because the healer was seeing someone. We sat on the veranda, and I noticed a boy around five years old. He was poking a black cat sitting on a chair with a wooden dagger.

"Don't do that," I said.

He kept poking the cat, without taking his deep, dark eyes off me. I raised the camera. A flash. The boy poked even more, and the cat meowed and jumped under the stable. He took a green apple off the table, chewed it and started walking up and down, with the apple clenched in his teeth, and a wooden dagger in his hand. His eyes flashed. I took one shot after another.

"Amochka's child is just as handsome," said Zainap. "It's a shame he has no father..."

Ama blushed.

"Goal!" came shouts from the yard.

I went over to the window.

Women were standing by the porch, and a little further away, in the meadow, children were kicking a ball. I took photos of them. They shouted excitedly:

"Terek is the champion!"

"Here you go!"

"Pass!"

"You missed!"

It was interesting that they were shouting in Russian, here, in the remote Vedeno region – the most untamable, the homeland of Basaev. Football. Oh yes, Chechnya beat TSSKA yesterday. Chechnya or Nokhch. Children of Noah.

"This land is inhabited by children," I thought. "How expressive the children here are! Children are the most important people here!"

There were many of them, terribly many. I recalled the crowd in Grozny. Teenagers stared furiously. A woman carried a baby, and it had an attentive flickering gaze, as if it were afraid to spill it. In the cloudy gazes of old men the teenagers' rage flickered with sun rays, and then their eyes would fade away again and become calm, like little children.

"How is my Vanechka in Moscow?" I thought – and my heart sank.

The healer could now see us, a lady in black flashed by us, and she picked up the large-eyed boy who by that time was already sucking on the apple core.

Zainap, Ama and I entered a dark, warm room.

A BOOK WITHOUT PHOTOGRAPHS

The healer was relatively young. He was a broad-shouldered, heavy-set man. He had greying black stubble on his face.

"Where are you from?" He looked at me simply, kindly, but also powerfully.

"From Moscow, he's a writer, a well-known one," Zainap said.

"Pleased to meet you. I'm Magomed. A former paratrooper. I'm forty-eight years old." He spoke in broken-off phrases, but not harshly, rather smoothly, falling off at the end. "I've always lived here. I've never been to Moscow. I'm a peaceful person. My wife died in the bombing, my son stayed with me. Since then my visions began. At night I can see what will happen tomorrow, and in a month, and in a year. I started to heal people. You love children, don't you?"

"Yes, I do," in surprise I grabbed the camera, but didn't dare to take any photos.

"You have a son, am I right?"

"Yes, a son."

"You'll have another son, and a daughter. I have a son too. Once soldiers came to me at night. "You're feeding rebels! Come with us, we'll shoot you." I replied: "I feed everyone. Whoever knocks on the door and asks for food, I give it to everyone." They took me away. My son woke up, he was twelve years old. He came running out and hugged me. They pushed him away, they dragged me and beat me with the butt of the gun, and drove my son away. There was a truck waiting. "Get in!" I got in. My son followed me. One soldier suddenly started shooting. At the stones, by my son's feet. My son ran away, the stones went flying and hit his feet. They held me for two days, and beat me. They let me go. I went home. It was quiet. My son was lying there, neither dead nor alive. His face was buried in the pillow. I shouted to him: "Malik!" He came to: "Dad? Alive?" Let me hug you… He's an adult now, time flies. He went to Pyatigorsk, he studies at the medical academy.

Magomed got up, mumbled a prayer mentioning Allah, went behind Zainap's back, ordered her to close her eyes and began to move his large hands, without touching her.

"Can I take a photo?" I asked.

"Yes, but be careful," he snorted and under the onslaught of flashes he said: "Your liver is sore. Bile. Congestion. Stones. Is that right?"

"Yes," the woman said.

"You'll live! What else? You don't sleep at night. You think. You're very sad. You feel miserable. Don't worry. The person you are crying for is in heaven."

The woman's shoulders shuddered, tears streamed out of her closed eyelids, and she buried her face in her hand.

"That's all. Now you. Sit down."

Zainap and I changed places. The chair she had been sitting on was hot. I obediently shut my eyes, and heard the caring voice:

"You fought a lot as a child. You fell down. But you didn't break anything. You played sport as a child. You gave it up a long time ago. Pump up your muscles. Don't turn to jelly. You'll get a cold. You need to keep your neck warm. Is that right?"

"Yes."

"You recently had a shock. But you'll endure. You've already gotten over it. You should talk less. Don't shout. You won't prove anything by shouting. You've got a weak throat. Are you a writer? Then you should write!"

I heard his laughter, opened my eyes, and Ama was laughing, bashfully and broken, and Zainap's face was wet. I also laughed, lightheartedly and foolishly, like in childhood.

We said goodbye laughing. With a laugh he rejected the money I offered him. With a laugh he shouted:

"Next! To the doctor!"

Laughing, we walked in single file along the edge of the muddy path, walking over the small stones, the same ones that the soldier had shot at, I thought, and they went flying, hitting the legs of the twelve-year-old kid.

The taxi was waiting for us. Off we drove.

"We're being followed," the driver said indifferently.

"Oh dear," Zainap said dully.

Ama looked petrified.

A red car raced in front of us, honked and flashed its lights. In the middle of the clear sunny day, the flash of headlights looked ridiculous.

We stopped on the side of the road. Silence.

Suddenly I got out, even surprising myself.

A man climbed out of the car, with a gun, in camouflage clothes, with a knife in his belt. He had a ginger beard, a bare skull and a harsh squint.

"Where are you from?'

"Moscow," I said, almost silently, and looked around for some reason.

Around me were mountains green with forests.

"And how's Moscow? Still standing?"

"Yes."

He scratched his nose with the index finger of his left hand (his right index finger was on the trigger of the gun):

"I was in Moscow, in 1990, when I was still a kid. Who are you?"

"A writer."

"Do you write poems, writer? Do you know Timur Mutsuraev?"

"Yes. I've heard of him. He's one of your singers."

"What song do you like?"

By his intonation, I understand that the ginger-bearded guy was a fan of Timur, and my memory suddenly and faithfully came up with the simple lines:

"The Afghan doesn't joke anymore, and Jaguar's not in this world, Aslan left with a smile, forever bathed in light…"

The ginger-bearded guy bared his teeth happily. And then he questioned me again.

"What were you doing here?"

"I went to a healer."

"To the wizard. He's a sinner. Are you going to write about him?"

"Yes."

"What's that you've got there. Give it to me." He took the camera. "You shouldn't take photos here."

"I write. And take photos," I said suddenly.

"So take the camera off. Give it here."

I quickly lifted the strap over my head, and he took the camera into his right hand, weighing it. He threw the gun over his shoulder. With his fingernail he pulled back the lid and took out the camera card.

"There!" he held out the camera, empty. "We're not thieves." And he repeated with emphasis: "You just shouldn't take any photos here. Ok, off you go."

I got into the taxi. "He let me go," I said, and the driver drove off. Zainap said something quietly in Chechen. Ama was petrified the whole way. Fear made her even more attractive.

"I'm not scared of anything," the driver said when we were back in Grozny. "When Allah wants to, He will call me".

The taxi driver was an unattractive guy in old dark clothes.

"Did you like the healer?" Umar asked over supper. "I tell you: it's all devilry. Although I saw a mermaid when I was young. In exile in Kazakhstan. I was riding my horse, and there was a naked woman with long hair, grey hair, sitting on a pole and laughing at me. I went flying off my horse out of fear."

Umar delved into his memories. Mystical stories of childhood and terrifying episodes from the war mixed together, as they do in stories told by boys.

"My father explained my fears to me," Umar said. "It's the shivering of your courage". In order not to be a coward, do you know what you should not be afraid of?"

"Fighting?" Ama asked, and Zainap sighed by the

stove, where she was frying fish.

"Away with you!" Umar waved his hand without malice. "You shouldn't be afraid of living. We lived all those years expecting death to come every minute, and we got used to it."

"It's a shame about the photographs," I said.

"Be happy that he didn't take you away as well," Umar said.

"Of course!" Ama said, she had already had something to drink and blushed in her headscarf. She looked good, resembled a matryoshka doll.

At sunset I helped Umar.

On the metal ladder I handed him window glass, heavy and slippery. The sunset and the flame of the gas torch burning nearby were reflected in the glass. We were tipsy, but neither of us wanted to admit it. The glass slipped out of Umar's hands, flew past me and smashed in the concrete courtyard.

"For happiness!" Umar said the required phrase.

Ama came out of the house and started sweeping up. She didn't ask: "Who did it?" She didn't ask anything at all.

As she swept, she lifted her face for a few moments.

"What a shame that we will never be husband and wife!" I thought, seeing how beautiful she was.

"And we won't even kiss," I added.

SERGEI SHARGUNOV

In The War

After the ginger-bearded guy in Chechnya took the memory card out of my camera, the glossy magazine didn't take my article. "It won't be any good without photos".

I still didn't have a job, and I offered articles to various magazines, but they turned me down. But a few years ago, when I was still just a writer, all of these people were happy to see me, and tried to persuade me to write something for them themselves.

Months of refusals dragged by – from one month to the next. If I was printed, the next time I was informed, with either fear or offense: "Sorry, you can't write for us". I was invited to appear on television, a car was waiting for me outside, but when I had already put my shoes on, I got another call: "You can't appear on our channel." But – what idiocy – the same thing happened again twice, when I was invited to appear on television, and even the car that honked outside! I laughed. I said: "Better check beforehand!" "But everything's fine, you're a welcome guest..." And it all happened again, I was called back, the girl's voice that had told me everything was fine had become stern, as if they had discovered that I was a criminal...

Shortly before my birthday I was invited to an official radio station – to talk about literature. "I'll go," I thought. "Evidently they've left me in peace, it's a kind of birthday present". I was told that the broadcast with me had been cancelled by cell phone, when I was already at the station, and my pass was being carefully examined at the booth.

And then it was summer – and a real war began.

And I flew to the war. I borrowed money from friends, and off I went. Not on an assignment from anyone, but because I wanted to. I didn't have a camera with me, just a cell phone.

First I landed in Vladikavkaz, and from there I went to the Roki tunnel.

There was a crowd of refugees by the tunnel: women and children, they were waiting to be sent further on.

"Don't go there, it's hell," a woman with disheveled hair said. "In our village, some people are crying, and the others are laughing. I sat in the basement all night and cried, and my neighbor, a Georgian woman, went out early in the morning and shouted happily: "Milk! Who wants fresh milk?"

The cheerful milk was the bitterest memory of the Ossetian woman, whose knees were bloody, because she had crawled away, hiding behind rocks from a persistent sniper.

I bargained with the soldiers by the tunnel. I gave them 1,000 rubles, and they took me with them. After we passed through the dusty tunnel, we entered the land of war. I sat on the shells in a roaring armored vehicle, squashed by other soldiers, and in the narrow porthole I could see the black smoke of burning villages.

We stopped.

"A sniper," came a yell from above.

Everyone who was on the tank jumped into the hole, and it was shut, and it became impossible to breathe.

"A monstrous beast," I thought. "And I'm in its belly. We're in its belly, savage people. We've been swallowed. The beast crawls and rolls across ancient spaces. To fight with other beasts." Sweat poured over my eyes, the heat was thermal. "What do you care," I tried to take my mind away from it. "You lost. What are you afraid of? What have you got to lose? If you get blown up, then never mind"… "No, I don't mind," another voice joined in. "Let me die then, but in the fresh air, and not here, in the sweaty darkness…" The unknown! That was the hardest of all. I said prayers to myself. "Lord, have mercy!" I prayed. And I constantly repeated the first line of the prayer: "Hail Mary, full of grace!" We passed the shooting zone. Air entered the tank once more, and there was a little more space.

"A plane," came a shout from above.

And soldiers jumped back in again, someone kneed me in the stomach, and the hatch was closed.

We drove at great speed.

"We have to move quickly, then a bomb won't hit us," said a soldier, who was soaking wet, spraying sweat.

I closed my eyes and saw pictures. Was I fainting, or was it a terrible dream? I saw myself differently. Mainly young, and in the summer.

I was shoved and pushed away.

"What's this?" I asked with a disobedient tongue.

"Tskhinvali!"

I sat on the dust, on the shells.

It was victory day. The Georgians had just been routed. Georgia had begun to retreat.

There was no food and not enough water in the town, but there was wine. Sweet and strong, it flowed, washing away the blood. In the center of town, three exploded tanks let off farewell smoke. From a black window, an Ossetian woman, an actress at a local burnt-down theater, theatrically portrayed the death of the crew to me. Closer to the outskirts, in the "Dubovaya Roshcha" district, killed Georgian soldiers lay on the ground. "A negro!" a militia man pointed to one of the dead. Or perhaps a Georgian had darkened in the burning sun and become an African? From the dead soldiers, you could see that they had been running ahead. In their still bodies an impression had been left of a victorious attack. Equipped, burnt and unreal, they seemed like the bodies of extra-terrestrials. "Maybe I should photograph them?" I asked myself. But I didn't.

I returned to the center. I went into the burning hotel, and walked along the floors. I looked into the black squares of rooms burnt by tank attacks.

A BOOK WITHOUT PHOTOGRAPHS

A hospital. I walked through its endless cold basement, over bloody rags, among shifted desks and crushed stretchers, and on the sunny surface, in bright tents that reminding me of a camping expedition, injured people who were lying there, brought into the light. Among others, I noticed one Georgian with an indifferent face. It seemed that even in an unconscious state he knew that he was a prisoner.

The day was enveloped with the smell of corpses, bitter-sweet and nauseating... Hunger, lack of water, endless cigarettes, heat, the smoky hands of the militia man which broke off a piece of black bread... I remember locals coming up to me and hugging me: "Are you from Russia? Thank you!" and how some journalists recoiled from them, and one volunteer soldier from Rostov beamed, waving his gun...

I wandered down the smoky Stalin Street, and a man came towards me and called me to follow him. We went into a yard. And so I joined a team of militia men.

The hill from which shots had been fired at night was blue, and before this shots had been fired both day and night. One house, a one-story barn, had been destroyed by a direct hit by a shell, leaving only charred remains. Another larger building, two-storied, made of stone and divided into apartment, was intact, but darkened by smoke. In the entrance way there was a funeral feast and celebration going on at the same time. The entrance way was filled with men. Each one had a gun by his feet. A loud old woman sometimes came to talk to us. They all talked among themselves in their own language.

I remember that one guy was so overcome by wine and brotherhood that he suddenly turned pale, grimaced and pulled the bolt. He was shushed up. And then an old, grey, stubbled man, the one who had called me here, to them, suggested digging a grave for the pregnant woman next door who had been killed, by shrapnel in the garden, when a shell had blown up the barn. The body had to be brought from the morgue. He asked: "Who will help?" He then looked me over with drunken, attentive eyes.

"Don't go anywhere. Or you'll be photographed!" The old woman interjected.

"Who'll photograph us?" The man objected. "It's quiet now. Can't you hear: it's completely quiet?"

"There's a sniper," she said stubbornly.

"There was a sniper at night, he's asleep now…"

"Perhaps he's just woken up…"

"Stop your moaning!"

And they swore at each other in their own language.

I didn't inquire where the dead woman's husband was, and whether her relatives were alive. I never found out whether there really was a pregnant neighbor and she had to be brought back from the morgue. I tore myself away from the plastic bottle of wine that we were passing around, I got up from the steps of the entrance way, with heavy legs, and went out into the heat of the day. The man brought two spades, and we started digging.

Very soon, we stopped talking. Wet and blind from sweat, we dug and dug, sometimes I turned my face or body away from a fly in irritation, without letting the spade go, and probably I would have turned away in the first second in just the same way if I had been hit by a bullet from a nearby hill. But we were replaced, we returned to the cold of the entranceway, I sat on the steps and fell asleep before I knew it. I woke up, in a minute, or in half an hour, I shook my head, got up with an effort of willpower, took a gulp, said goodbye to everyone, went outside (the grave was still being dug) and left the courtyard, down the bullit-riddled Stalin Street.

My arms ached, and my mood was improving. No one photographed me. "It really is great that I'm alive!" I thought.

It was getting dark. In the headquarters of the Russian troops I ate some canned stewed meat. Chechens from the "East" battalion, bearded men, lined up for a hose that was firing a powerful jet of water, and washed their bare torsos, and went into their iron wagon. The Chechens had just returned from battle.

It got cold immediately. I went to sleep in some hall that resembled a gym. People were lying side by side. The floor was freezing cold. I huddled up, with my knees to my chin, put a sweater over myself, a bag under my head, and still shivered all night. I woke up from cold. A gun was echoing and a sniper was firing. A goat was bleating. A toad was complaining loudly.

All night I dreamt of Vanya, my son. As if he were riding on a large bed and yelling his favorite war cries: "Tarin-tatarin! Tarin-tarin-tarin! Dindlya! Bomblya! Tustik!" By morning, the child had turned into a kitten, for some reason.

In the morning, the dead were buried in the yards again, in the greenery, in flowers. Calm came, but chaos called. The wave of wanderers moved forward – from Ossetia into Georgia.

I wanted to see what was there, in that land. I left Tskhinvali. At the checkpoint was a Dagestani peacekeeper, ordering conscripts around. He gave us trophy Georgian beer. The checkpoint was a concrete box riddled with bullets, and with no glass. The entire previous night they were shot at. The Dagestani giggled nervously. He told us how the war began, and he went away, crawling, hiding in the wild grass, under the roar of firing.

"My friend," I said. "I want to go further!"

"A friend's request is law," he winked nervously.

And five minutes later he stopped a Zhiguli car.

"This is my friend!"

And so I found myself in a car filled with boys. Kids really, the age of senior high school pupils. They had flown to Georgia to celebrate the victory. I was given the place of honor – in front, next to the driver.

"Gori... I want Gori.... I've never seen what Gori looks like..." one dreamer sighed, and came up with a slogan: "Gory Gori!"

Georgia greeted us with decadent comfort. Meadows, vineyards, tennis courts, restaurants. The inscriptions, shaped like vines, were duplicated in English. From the first minutes, there was an aroma of fire. I stuck my head out the window and began to take photos with my cell phone.

The further we went, the thicker the smoke was, and the more cars there were, and guns stuck out of the cars, and shooting could be heard. Every car honked, from everyone a wild cry came – it was a sign of one's own people. An anticipation was felt in the stuffiness: when would we run into strangers?

We drove, and I looked attentively and clicked. A dead old man in a tracksuit in a shop entrance. I clicked and thought: the poor man. Then I thought: I wonder if the photo came out. I checked. No, it was blurry. Men were smoking at a gas station. Click. A man in camouflage jumped out of the vines, clutching his weapon, and snow-white chickens came running out from under his legs. Click.

I clicked, and looked at the result, and got to the photos of my son on the cell phone. And once more, I had got carried away. I kept photos of Vanya away from stranger's eyes, but I constantly photographed him. There he was standing in white and blue pajamas in his crib, and with his right hand he held the wooden bars. There he was smiling, with a touching haircut, and the squinting gaze of a little storyteller. There he was in a brown sweater, leaning forward, waiting for a signal to attack, his teeth bared, his eyes looking somewhere into the distance, his hair disheveled like grass: a real Nestor Makhno. And there he was in a fur coat and hat, simple but cunning, with a naughty and playful look, distracted by something else. He wanted to throw snow and run from snowdrift to snowdrift: "Hello, bear!", "Hello, camel!"

The driver howled. The breaks squealed.

A BOOK WITHOUT PHOTOGRAPHS

A tank emerged through the smoke. There were abandoned cars. On the asphalt, strangely tense, bodies lay. You got the impression that they were about to do push-ups. I started taking photos again through the windshield. My cell phone clicked constantly, as if it had lost its mind. It seemed to me that this constant clicking created a wall between my life and what was happening around me.

"Why did you kill people," someone shouted.

"I didn't kill anyone…"

We were surrounded by men with guns. I slowly got out.

"Russian?" the officer looked distrustfully from the tank. "A cell phone? Nokia? Great! Listen, where you are calling? No one will help you… You can't go any further, you hear."

My companions were placed face-down on the asphalt with the rest.

The officer looked like the singer Garik Sukachev.

"We're kind, we protected them. We're fighting America here. Listen, take the monkey!"

Hunched over, a swarthy man in a blue singlet came out from behind the tank. Through the darkness of his face, the white of fear could be seen. He held out a crumpled piece of paper to me. Written on it were the words: "Who is right / guilty? The Russians? The Georgians? The Ossetians? Don't know?" He was conducting a survey.

"Where are you from?"

He raised his black eyebrows in the style of Mr. Bean.

"Where are you from?"

"Brazil! Brazil!"

"The freak ran away from Georgia," one of the soldiers said.

A guy came over to the tank, bringing a girl with him. He frantically squeezed her tits, to explain that she was his. A Georgian couple. The officer let them through, in the direction of Gori.

Shooting was heard from somewhere nearby. The Russians hid in the tank. The Ossetians jumped out. The shooting stopped.

It's a separate story about how I covered the road back to Tskhinvali with the Brazilian.

Hours later, dazed from smoke, fire and shooting, we were picked up in a trophy BMW by Russian special service officers.

They told a lot of jokes, they were good guys.

At high speed they knocked the windscreen out with their gun-butts.

I crouched down, and the Brazilian roared. His cheek had been cut.

War is a mess. I'm sure any war is. Even the fairest one. When you've been present at a war, you feel shame. As if you're guilty. You leave, and they stay behind, everyone you've seen.

You can't say a lot of words about a real war.

How I Fired My Friend

I couldn't stay in one place.

I realized what the problem was. Like the hero of a fairy-tale, I was looking for the truth. I wanted to find out something important, in order to go on living.

And so I went away again. Outside the train window, the bloodless landscape of northern Russia extended: swamps and bushes. At the stops, white northern dogs came running up, with protruding ribs, and barked at us, lifting their martyr-like snouts.

I arrived in Severodvinsk at sunset. I was met by my friend Andryukha, and his friend Edik. Andryukha was a handsome blue-eyed man with high cheekbones, and a calm face. Edik was almost an Albino, tall, and constantly jumping up and down. He jumped as he waited on the platform, and jumped on the way to the car, as if he was being pulled up into the sky.

We went into a bar and ordered a carafe of vodka, meat and pickles. Edik began to describe the nightmares of his construction business.

"Sergun, you're here at last: you should go there," he leaned over to me across the table. "Listen to people, write down what they say… I read you! Remember, I sent you a letter when you were removed from the elections! 'Lenin, Solovki' – that was me."

"He was born on the Solovki Islands," Andrei said.

"Why are you Lenin, though?" I asked.

"If you travel across all of Russia, no one and nothing will stop you," Edik continued. "No one will say a bad word about you. I saw it on the Internet: they were so angry that they didn't have any power over you! They write that you're a drug addict, ha ha. I read your book "Hooray!" It's quite the opposite – for a healthy life. I gave up smoking after "Hooray!", and started jogging."

"That's true," Andrei nodded.

"When I found out that you'd been removed from the elections, I started smoking again." In confirmation, Edik pulled a cigarette out of the packet and turned it between his fingers. "Sergun, they can't forbid meeting with you. These are meetings between readers and the writer..." he dropped the cigarette. It rolled across the table and stopped on the edge.

"Lenin?" I asked again. "Why are you Lenin, though?"

"I used to lisp, in kindergarten. Then I stopped, but the nickname stuck! I didn't lisp at school, but they still called me Lenin. You know yourself: one person said it, and everyone repeated it!" he banged his hand on the table, and the cigarette dropped into the abyss.

"This is a small town," Andrei agreed mysteriously.

"And now I'm going bald..." Edik stroked his head.

After supper we went our separate ways: Edik walked home to his wife and baby daughter, and I went to Andryukha's house. Although we went in different directions, both identical fog and wind awaited both Edik and us on the way home. The sea, which could not reach us with the water, drove enormous waves of wind across the streets.

Andrukha also had a daughter, in fact, but he had been living alone for half a year now. His wife had gone to live with a local dentist and took their eight-year-old daughter with her.

We sat in the kitchen over a yellowed blue tablecloth and drank tea. We talked about literature. Andrei was a critic and columnist, he wrote for a lot of publications. For half a year now, he had been working in the press-service of city deputies, which is how he made a living. In the two days I was in town, he had been given time off, his boss was understanding, and interested in books. "I'll introduce you tomorrow," said Andrei, and we changed the subject to his family troubles.

"She didn't fall in love with him, she fell in love with his money... I'm not poor either, but how can I compete with a dentist? To hell with her. It's a shame she hid my daughter away. I haven't seen my Katya for a month, they just won't let me see her. I was about to go to court, and suddenly I ran into them: my wife and that bastard... This is a small town. I met them in a restaurant." Andrei talked in a humble voice. His face remained kind and motionless. "I went up to him and said: 'Get up'. He got up, and I knocked his teeth out."

"All his teeth."

"A lot of them... A lot of teeth," Andrei chuckled for the same time. "Imagine, I knocked out a dentist's teeth. With one punch."

I quickly glanced at my friend's hands: large and soft, they harmlessly and even mournfully lay by the tea cup, from which steam was rising.

"You're strong..."

"No, we're the same build, you and I. Anger gave me strength. I wanted to beat him up. But look what happened, I had to pay for him to get new teeth."

"Did he implant them himself, I wonder?"

Andrei replied with a modest curse – to say that he didn't know.

"They took my daughter away a week ago. To Gatchina, near Petersburg. They've moved there. I'll take a vacation and go and visit her there." He sipped from the cup and fell silent, deep in thought, as if savoring the boiling water. "What about you? Do you see your son?"

"Yes, I do."

"You didn't smooth things over with Anya?"

"Not particularly."

"I see."

The next morning we went to the factory. We were accompanied by a taciturn, squat man. This FSB man was supposed to supervise our movements around the factory. He made sure that we didn't take any photographs. The main secret of the factory was that it was only working at half of its capacity, at best. But it was still wonderful, magnificent here! The workers still worked here – at this Sevmash factory, which was built by prisoners on the site of an old monastery among marshlands.

I walked around the three-storey workshop, and a board went flying under foot. The enormous barge towered, hemmed in by wooden passages, in the noise and racket, among the flashes of the electrical welders, which reminded me of the paparazzi. In the air the dock was waiting for it, to where it would go before moving further – into the White Sea.

In the factory port, caressed by the sea water, two more boats towered. They were being rebuilt for India. The FSB guy mumbled: "Don't go any further", but a moment later misery covered his face, he waved a dry hand, and we went closer.

The iron hulk stood black against the background of the cool, dreary sunny day.

Workers in blue coats were hurrying towards the hulk. Dark-haired and blond, boys and girls, they argued enthusiastically, roughly, and laughed in a friendly way. Salt of the earth! There was some participation in the mysteries in their delight. "Perhaps in the mystery of death?" I asked myself, and replied: "Hardly!"

I noticed one girl: she had a lavender headscarf, and a black forelock. She was brazen and cheerful, nourished with atomic radiation, and was laughing and running with the others. Suddenly I felt her superiority, my weakness because I could not stop her, and ask her out on a date. She was inaccessible. As she marched towards the secret insides, the iron depths, surrounded by her fellow workers. But what stopped me? Why couldn't I get to know her, if she was pretty?

"Hey! Hi!"

She looked over her shoulder, interested, without surprise. She must have realized that I was shouting to her.

"Don't talk to the personnel," the FSB man took me by the elbow.

A BOOK WITHOUT PHOTOGRAPHS

The workers went off into the distance.

Outside the factory, Edik was waiting for Andrei and me. He looked fresh and was eating an ice cream. We got into his car.

"Well then Lenin, how are you?" I asked.

"You know who you are? I worked it out. I couldn't sleep last night, my daughter was crying, and I worked out what your name was. Your first name rhymes with your surname! Didn't you know! Sergun Shargun! How's that?" He took his hands off the steering wheel and clapped. "Huh?"

"You're a cheerful bunch here in Severodvinsk," I said. "Maybe it's because of a lack of oxygen?"

"We have two states of being: we sleep or laugh," Andrei said.

"Sometimes we laugh in our sleep," Edik said.

We arrived at the main newspaper in town, where I was welcomed with alarm and curiosity, by the editor-in-chief, who was small, chubby, and smart. The entire editorial staff was gathered there, mainly large women and skinny girls. We were all photographed together. "You know, our city used to be called Molotovsk," the editor-in-chief confided to me.

After this there was a meeting at another newspaper, which was freer. But the staff turned out to be just the same as in the last one: well-fed women and thin girls. The editor-in-chief resembled a wild boar. When I got a better look at him, I realized that his stubble was disguising scars, and that one eye under the glass of his smoky glasses was covered in a pink membrane.

"What's he look so battered for?" I whispered to Andrei.

"He was attacked in his doorway," my friend explained in a whisper. "He was all cut up..."

Then we went to the site. In a brick cottage, I was recorded on video for the city's Internet site. Yesterday's TV channel had turned into a site. The owner, a bearded man called Vlas, was gloomy. His shapely wife called Marta came out of the cottage, a nervous blond woman with bright lips and nails. They said that the channel had been blocked, and that so far the site got 100 visitors a day. They had to start life again from scratch. I drank a glass of whiskey with Vlas, and Andrei and Edik joined in, even though he was driving.

"I always drink without ice," Vlas hissed. "Why bother with ice? Do real men drink it with ice?"

Only now did I notice that he was deep in the middle of a drinking bout.

"I'm a man, and I drink it with ice, and so what?" Edik asked impudently.

The blond woman looked at them with burning eyes, as if they were about to fight, and not over the ice, but over her. But nothing happened.

The next stop was the university. The philology department. The lecturer (a friend of Andrei and Edik), young, dashing, with turned-up black whiskers, had a full lecture hall. Almost all of the students were female.

I told them a few stories about the literary profession. I recalled how I had once seen an ad on television for the "Debut" prize, and sent them a love story in a large yellow envelope and won, beating 40,000 competitors. And before that, I recalled, when I was not yet able to read, I was already writing – I would take books and copy the letters. And even before that, at the age of two, I jumped up and down in the cradle at night and cried in response to the yellow light shining through the blinds: "The moon lives in my window. It is so very hard!"

And I offered to be friends with everyone on Odnoklassniki, VKontakte and Facebook. I knew this was the best method for gaining new allies. Many of them took out their phones immediately and hunched over them, evidently going online and sending friend requests.

"Could I ask you..." when the young crowd had drifted away with a roar, a girl approached me. "I want to write fairy-tales. I already have everything in my head, but nothing on paper yet." She was wearing a black T-shirt, had black hair and black lips, as if she had been eating blueberries.

"Are you a Goth?" I winked.

"No. I want to be an Emo."

"You want to?"

"That's Lyuba Pastukhova," the lecturer said. "There are some real originals here! She read Boris Shergin, our unforgettable storyteller, and fell in love with fairy-tales."

"Can I talk to you?" The girl looked at me keenly and faithfully.

She was charming and soft-skinned. Her vulnerability was only emphasized by those blueberry lips.

"Come to the pub in the evening," Edik said. "Do you know *Belomorye*? That's the one. There at eight."

"Will you tell me about fairy-tales?" She looked me straight in the eyes.

"We'll tell you, and show you," Andrei replied with a dull laugh.

"Don't drink too much," the lecturer ruffled her hair, with a jealous gesture, it seemed to me: out of the black thicket a blue tress fell down.

Andrei, Edik and I decided to go for a walk until the evening.

The wind was growing stronger. The wind lifted up garbage and scattered it around.

The wind was blowing – back and forth, one squall after another. It stopped for a moment, but then blew in sideways, from around the corner, powerful and destructive, like a cavalry of ghosts. The stone five-story buildings, dilapidated, many with peeling paint (green, for some reason), looked wild. Their walls and corners spoke of the unrelenting and rough caresses of the wind from the sea. These poor buildings looked malevolent! They were caressed and tormented, mauled and hacked. Ghosts fought ghosts over every building. These poor, poor building, that belonged to the winds, and not to people!

We turned up at Belomorye when it was only half past six, not quite ourselves because of the wind.

And so, by eight o'clock our table was already excitable and boisterous. We were united by a despair of unknown origin. Edik told us about the mess in the construction business, then about women, swearing more and increasingly harshly with each glass he drank. Andrei gave in and smoked a cigarette, although he hadn't smoked in ten years. Unable to withstand the feeling of misery, I also smoked.

Lyuba turned up at eight on the dot. She was wearing a blue jumper, and her lips weren't dark, but the conventional pink color.

"Hello hipsters!" Edik took her by the shoulders and sat her down.

"Don't be rude," said Andrei.

She started asking me about fairy-tales, paying no attention to Andrei or Edik. She licked her lips slowly and widely, probably overcoming embarrassment. What fairy-tales did I read as a child, did I like fairy-tales now, did I write them for my son or did I read him ones by other people?

"I have to leave tomorrow," I said. "Do you know Andrei? He knows a lot about literature. And you live in the same city. Talk to him…"

"I added you in Odnoklassniki. Can I write to you?"

"Do you write fairy-tales?" Andrei asked. "Hey!" he poked her. "I said: fairy-tales?"

"Yes," she said, and turned to me, taking me in with her greedy eyes.

I pictured to myself: I would leave, and I would be attacked by texts and messages on the Internet. And then she would get angry… The girl had to live here, in this windblown city, and we probably wouldn't see each other again.

I shifted my eyes to my friend. He knocked back a

glass, wiped his lips with his fist, with a broad gesture, as if he were rehearsing a punch to knock some teeth out. If I responded to her attention, and we slept in Andrei's bachelor apartment, where the voices of his wife and daughter recently were heard, there would be some warm and murky nastiness in this. My friend needed her more – that was it!

"Do you like Andersen?" Lyuba drawled in a begging voice.

"Ask Andrei," I suddenly got up from the table and went to the men's room.

When I came back, they had a satisfied and absent look, as if they had just been kissing. My friend, with a red face, a shirt with three of the buttons undone, was hugging the ruddy-faced lover of fairy-tales and muttering something quietly, and she giggled, moved away a little and then moved back. She didn't look at me. She shot a look at me with a green eye – a bullet of loathing – and giggled again, repeating: "Yes?", "Really?" "What are you saying…" The drastic change that had taken place in her while I was in the men's room galled me somewhat.

"Lyuba, do you remember Andersen," I said playfully, "The girl who stepped on the bread?"

She kept listening to my friend, as if all other sounds had disappeared for her.

"Lyuba-a!" I raised my voice.

"No!" She said angrily.

"What do you mean no?"

"What do you want? Get lost."

Andrei, grinning blissfully, pressed her to himself more decisively.

"Trash. Bitch," I mumbled into the glass and knocked it back in one gulp.

"Lyuba, are you angry with me?"

"Don't be jealous, pal," Edik leaned over to me across the table. "Let them sweet-talk each other." He lowered his voice. "Andryukha's having a hard time at the moment, you might have women coming out of your ears in Moscow, but here…"

"This is a small town," Andrei said, talking about something of his own, Lyuba giggled, and Edik, snickering, gave me a teasing look:

"There you go!"

"Oh," Andrei became stern, and pulled back his arm that lay between the sofa and the girl, and started to get up: "Boris Stepanovich…"

A lanky man in a grey suit was grinning, attentively and shortsightedly looking over the table, and asked in a broken voice:

"Are you celebrating, youngsters?"

He and Andrei hugged. His friend flung open his arms and threw himself at the jacket, as if he were jumping into the sea. From the side of the jacket, a narrow yellow hand slapped Andrei on the back.

Then the yellow hand was extended to me, and the broken voice said:

"I'm very glad to meet you. I'm Andrei's boss. I've heard a lot about you."

At the sight of the new person, Edik fell silent. Perhaps through his increasing drunkenness he realized that he shouldn't make a noise in front of his friend's boss.

"Right, I'm off! My daughter's crying. She can't get to sleep without her dad," he threw a banknote on to the table and went away to cough.

"Lenin," Andrei sighed, and Lyuba giggled.

After a little while, three more people joined the table: two guys who worked with Andrei, one of them with his wife. They were quite modest.

"It's good that you travel. Where have you been?" Boris Stepanovich asked amiably.

"Almost everywhere. Chechnya. Ossetia."

"That's very interesting. Well then, are the plagues of Egypt over? People aren't bothering you? I also suffered in my youth. I wrote poems. One of them was very hot for those times! They wanted to expel me from the Komsomol."

"Can I take your picture?" a round, shaven-headed guy asked, leaving his wife at the table, a chubby dyed blonde, whom I moved closer to.

He clicked the camera.

"Closer," he shouted.

His wife's breast touched me through her blouse. For some reason I squeezed her knee. She didn't try to get away. I moved my fingers up her knee.

"Closer, people," the guy called. "Che-e-ese!"

I wanted more – to grab his wife's breast.

Andrei smiled more broadly than everyone else, blissfully, like a traitor. He was silent, frowning, and suddenly Lyuba, who was probably drunk by now, started to caress him and lick his ear with a lithe tongue.

"You don't face pressure?" Boris Stepanovich continued. "You're not oppressed?"

"Everything's fine, more or less," I said. "I hope its fine. Why?"

"Andrei's a good guy. He's going to be promoted. He did well! He invited you to come here! Have you already had meetings? At newspapers? How are our students?"

"Student girls," I said and looked at Lyuba.

She was also looking at me: out of the corner of her eye as she continued to kiss and lick my northern friend's ear, red and with a ripe lobe. No, there wouldn't be any hostility. Andrei was turning red all over – his face, his ears, his chest where his shirt was open – from embarrassment, pleasure, drink, or everything at once.

I looked away and drank again.

"She's a Goth," I said with difficulty. "You know, Goths – they're like hoodlums…"

Boris Stepanovich frowned in understanding.

"Oh, she's not a Goth," I corrected myself. "She's an emo!"

"Young people play games, and the echo even reaches our village," Boris Stepanovich replied poetically, with a scratch and a squint.

That evening he didn't drink, and didn't even eat anything.

It was dark and windy, and only the three of us remained.

"You're a fine girl! I thought you were weird or something," Andrei mumbled. "But you're so cool! I thought you were a bit crazy, but you're quite OK!" He turned to me and hissed: "You're not angry?" And plunged his face into hers.

They kissed, risking falling down.

"I forgot my cell phone," I remembered. "Wait."

I ran back, against the wind. I raced into the restaurant. The music was five times louder than it had been before.

Our table was already empty.

"My phone! I lost it!" I yelled, rushing over to the bar.

The woman at the bar, bony, blond, in a white shirt, shook her head and stretched her lips:

"We don't have it…"

I silently opened my mouth with bad words.

My cell phone had a lot of photos on it. Of the Ossetian war. Of my son. It had been stolen…

Damn you all. "They probably turned the music up to hide the trace," I thought drunkenly and rushed away from the bar to the exit. But what if my friend had already vanished into the darkness with Lyuba? What should I do? What could I do without a telephone? Look for a hotel? Did I have enough money? I thought all of this as I went out into the darkness, but they hadn't gone anywhere.

The two of them swayed, stuck together in a kiss, bathed in the blue light of the restaurant sign.

"My telephone's been stolen."

"Never mind!" Andrei surfaced from the kiss, and Lyuba giggled, almost quacked.

Next to his house, Andrei went into a bodega and bought a bottle of champagne. He waved it around for a long time. The cork went flying into the darkness and was carried away.

He took a long slug and gave the bottle to his girlfriend. Lyuba swallowed and gave it to me.

"No thanks!" I said.

In the apartment we immediately separated. Andrei went to his room to lie down, Lyuba and went off to the bathroom.

I sat down in the other room and settled down on the Internet.

Without getting up off the chair and tearing myself away from the monitor, I took my clothes off. On the Odnoklassniki site, nineteen female students from Severodvinsk and four male students wanted to be my friends.

While I was confirming their friendship and reached the swarthy virtual Lyuba, I could hear her taking a shower, and then she waddled from the bathroom to Andrei.

"Do you have condoms?" She asked loudly.

"Hi! You're so nice! Thanks for that! See you soon!" she wrote to me on the Internet. The message was sent at 19:19, less than an hour was left before she came to the restaurant, where Andrei would get her.

Through the wall her cries and sighs could be heard.

Was she moaning that loudly on purpose? So I could hear? Why did she want to do that?

I got up and walked from the shuttered window to the door. Behind the glass of the cupboard, among the tea service, there were paper squares: the insides of greeting cards from a little girl to her father, for his birthday and the New Year. They had clearly been written before the family fell apart. "Papa, I love you! Be well and love mama and me!" Square letters, written in different colored pencils, some of them pointing the wrong way....

Would this girl write this to you now?

I turned off the computer. I got undressed and lay down with my face to the wall, through which the northern cries of the student could still be heard, monotonous and miserable. I fell asleep immediately.

I was woken by noise. I jumped off the bed, placed the bedding in two even piles, like a soldier, and went to the kitchen in my underpants. Andrei was sitting at the table, in a dark blue suit and a pink tie.

"Oh, you're all dressed up!" I whistled. "Are you off to the marriage office? Where's the bride?"

"She just left. I'm going to work."

"But you've got a day off…"

"I've got some problems."

"What's wrong?"

"My boss just called. He said: 'You've got problems.'" My friend poured the remains of the champagne from the bottle into the cup, drank it and frowned: it was flat.

"Nonsense," I said. "He's a decent guy, your boss."

"Was I rude to him yesterday? Was everything OK?"

"It was fine," I said, and the prickly words reminded me that I wanted some water.

"Were you rude to him, Sery?"

"No, I wasn't. Do you have any water, Andryukha?"

"There's some cold water in the kettle." My friend got up. "I'll go and find out what's going on, and you wait here?"

"How was Lyuba? Charming?"

He waved his hand feebly, and the door slammed. Drinking the water greedily, from the fifth floor window I saw his fine figure, which was swiftly moving down the grey street, chased and overtaken by the wind, further and further….

He returned two hours later. He went into the kitchen and sat down. His face was waxen and motionless.

He raised the cup, shook it, and indifferently drank the flat champagne:

"I've been fired."

"Why?"

"He said he got a phone call."

"Where from?"

"He said he got a phone call: 'Is Shargunov in town? Are you receiving him?'"

"That's insane," I said, tired. "What do they hate me for?"

"Now they hate me too," Andrei sighed, "I've never seen my boss like that before. He had eyes like a mad cockroach: 'Did you invite Shargunov? Do you even know who he really is? Say goodbye to your job!'" He didn't even shake my hand. He called Kolyan, our co-worker, he was there with his wife yesterday. He said: 'Where's the camera?' 'At home.' 'Go straight home then. Bring it to my office, and we'll delete all the photos with Shargunov. In my presence. So I can see it.' And he gave me a piece of paper and a pen. 'Put the date and your signature, fuck it,' and didn't look at me. 'Screw you,' I said. 'You're shitting yourself, aren't you?' I said. I signed the paper and went out. To hell with that job…."

A few hours later, Andrei, Edik-Lenin and I were sitting on an overturned boat on a wild beach of Severodvinsk and drinking vodka. Between us on the overturned boat bottom were our comrades – plastic cups and a torn-open packet of salami.

It was low tide. In the distance was the dark sea, the sun murkily lit the dunes, fir trees and the red star of someone's heroic grave that was situated right on the beach.

"I'd like to be buried by the sea," I said. "In the sand. It's probably not so good for the corpse, and the pit will get washed away, but it's beautiful: a grave by the sea shore."

"Everything will be OK with the coffin," Edik said. "Like with this boat. It's been here for several years. It's rotting from the moisture, of course. But it's also become salted. It's getting stronger. That's the dialectic, damn it…" he stroked the rough wood.

The boat wisely smiled with every crack and gap.

"Fuck it all," Andryukha said. "Pour the vodka!"

"Don't you want to call Lyuba?" I asked.

"Fuck Lyuba… What about you?"

"My cell phone was stolen. Did you forget?"

"You should block it," Edik said sensibly.

"I should," I said.

"Thank you, Seryozha!" Andrei said. "I thought I wouldn't see Katya until autumn. But I'll see her in a few days! They fired me, Seryozha, they fired me because of you, don't worry, brother. Now I'm free! I'm free, you understand? I'll go to see my daughter in Gatchina! I'm not an idiot: while I had a job, I saved money. I'll go there and rent a house, and go and work as a teacher at the school. You'll see, I'll teach Katya…"

I left that evening.

The lingonberry sunset stretched over the swamp. The conductor in the train car was an old drunk travelling with a black, well-fed cat. Skinny white dogs ran around the train at the stops. From the platform I saw the cat looking out the window. The dogs looked up and yelped miserably, as if they were asking the cat for help.

The cat looked at them through the glass, somewhat puffed up.

I travelled to Moscow and knew that my friend would leave Severodvinsk the following day.

Revolution In Asia

I had never seen a revolution before.

You can live your entire life and never see a revolution.

Time passed by, and I slowly but surely recovered... I began to be printed again by various newspapers and magazines. With some reservations, but more and more willingly... I had a book published. The publisher signed a contract for a second book. I started to have money.

When the news said there were disturbances and shootings in Kyrgyzstan, I immediately called Seva.

He was a progressive European. A hipster. He worked at a cultural website, where he wrote an article once a month. The rest of the time he spent in the warm darkness of clubs, drank tea and squinted at the only source of light – the monitor of his laptop with the twitter feed.

He always carried a bulky camera with him, loaded with black and white film. His photos were crippled – blurred around the edges. Seva thought that this was beautiful and unusual. He usually took photos pointing the camera upwards: the sky, branches, walls and roofs.

His relaxed life did not stop him from travelling to Asia. He had already been to Kyrgyzstan and Uzbekistan, had spent a long time there, and knew the customs. And he knew where to stay. So when the troubles began in Kyrzgystan, I called him:

"Let's go to Kyrgzystan, Seva!"

"Let's go..." he replied modestly.

Seva was not a coward. If you offered him to fly to Mars, he would agree without any doubts or nervousness. He would reluctantly close his laptop, hang his prehistoric camera around his neck, yawn and go to the spaceship. Fearless and sluggish, he was actually just very calm.

But I needed Kyrgyzstan and its revolution as the last confirmation that I was needed in this life. I decided to test fate a third time. But I flew there quite serenely, for some reason knowing for certain that I was needed, I wouldn't be killed, and I would return.

And of course, I wanted terribly to see what it looked like when the revolution triumphed.

Seva was packed into a widened striped shirt, narrow jeans and sizeless sneakers. Long brown bangs hung down on his forehead.

"Are you going there looking like that?" I asked.

"What's wrong with that?" he looked surprised. "There are people there like this too."

"Where's your camera?"

He nodded at an orange cloth bag over his arm.

The plane landed in darkness. It taxied for a long time, rolling over an uneven runway, without any lights, and finally stopped.

At the airport, the people in military jackets looked watchfully. Their narrow eyes showed an icy efficiency, and their movements were sudden and sparing.

From the airport we took a taxi to Bishkek, where Seva's acquaintances had already prepared an apartment for us.

The road was covered in potholes. The old "Volga" bounced up and down with a crash, and around us misty dawn fields lay stretched out.

"Tan," said Seva. "Tan means dawn in Kyrgyz".

The driver turned around:

"We're friends with the Russians, without the Russians would be like being without ears."

"You're driving so fast," I said. "Aren't you afraid of traffic police?"

"They should be scared now. The cops have gone into hiding. Did you hear what they did to the head cop? That was in Talas. He hid in a dug-out pit. They caught him, beat him, and turned him into pulp. They threw him off the second floor twice."

We drove into the city, which revealed Soviet ivory buildings emerging from the lilac fog. The first ray of sunlight came shining through. Greetings, lost outskirts of the Empire!

In the morning light I read the street signs as the car drove past them. "Aelita" hair salon. "Retro-metro" bar and café. A shop called "Meat and Bread". In Russian.

"Everyone speaks Russian here!" the driver guessed what I was thinking. "There's no escaping it. Do you know what else happened to Kognatiev?"

"Who?"

"The head cop of yours. He had a nightstick shoved in his backside. A police one. Tagdyr…"

"What?"

"Fate," Seva translated with melancholy.

Kyrgyz tagdyr – the second revolution had taken place five years after the first one.

Seva and I stood in the sun by the white government building with broken windows. The building had burnt up to the seventh floor. One window was special: a long black mark up the wall, evidently the flames had risen high.

On a stone bench, a guy in a leather jacket was waving an enormous heavy red flag, and panting, he yelled hoarsely. "This is our home," Seva translated. "Give it to the young. It will be our palace!"

There was a crowd milling about, 200 people or so. The guy jumped up and down. The hoarse voice of the prayer was turned on above the people, and they crouched down to remember those who had been killed.

The photographs of the slain were stuck to a black fence. They were almost all young. Russian faces were also among them. There were also leaflets. A handwritten poem in memory of a friend: "Bullets flew like fiery blizzards… Why did these blizzards appear on your body?"

A pale grey tent had been set up among the people. I squatted down, like everyone else, and looked in. A girl was sitting in the semi-darkness of the tent, and was hard to make out.

"Now I'm here…" she said dully, as if apologizing. "Where are you from, Osh?"

"No, Moscow."

The prayer ended, and the girl crawled out. She was small, in a bright cardigan, with a large mouth, and narrow eyes like canoes. Ayana was nineteen years old. She had come here from the city of Osh.

"Ayana in Kyrgyztsan, Ama in Chechnya, Anya in Russia," I thought.

The flowers on the ground, Ayana said, indicated the bodies of people killed the day before. "Look at the gate!" The gate of the white building was bent in an avant-garde style. "That's from the explosion of a grenade." The mutilated gate was covered with a play board picturing a classic oil painting – mountains, blue sky, a proud figure on a horse.

"Beautiful!" Seva photographed the gate.

The first people who ran to the gate were mowed down by bullets.

"Here," Ayana showed us. "An old man's eye lay here all day yesterday. The body and the eye were separate."

She pointed at the rich head of a crimson rose separate from the stem:

"Where the flower was laid, that's where the eye was. When we ran away under the shower of bullets, we jumped over the eye. When we triumphed, and started dancing, we protected the eye. It lay there, like a… uikzat…"

"Sacred relic," Seva translated. "When did you come here?"

Ayana fluttered her eyelashes, a sign of honesty:

"Yesterday after the storm. My brothers fought here, and they went home to rest. It was fierce! People from all over the country. They tortured us. We're sick of the bribes. For every sheep you need to buy a certificate. The country was looted. The people drove away the cops.

Then snipers started shooting. They shot from all the tall buildings. And people realized that they were being killed, they got angry and rose up like they were drunk. They pulled down the snipers and slit their throats. And they ran ahead, not back. They took the government building, the parliament, television... A guy showed a photo of Bakiev's photo on TV, turned around and said "Bitch!" They did it all themselves! There were no leaders... And then they thought about what to do with power. So they gave it to our opposition... But it's already making mistakes, this new government. Why did they let Bakiev flee? And the snipers weren't Kyrgyz. They say they were Chechens. Or Slavs." She broke up, looking at me and my friend in alarm. "You're not Chechens, are you?"

"Let me take a photograph of you," said Seva.

Ayana immediately forgot her alarm. We stood against the background of the mutilated gate. I put my arm around her shoulders.

"Are you journalists?" A thin young man with curly hair asked.

"Let me photograph you," Seva said to him softly.

The young man stood before the camera, blocking us. He spoke in the broken voice of an accuser:

"I'm a Dungan. We're Chinese, but Muslims. Write that down, please. Dungans. Different peoples shouldn't be made to quarrel among themselves. Dungans are good. Uighurs are good. Uzbeks aren't bad. Uzbeks are already being burnt alive."

"Sen yemneden korkosun?" Ayana asked haughtily.

"What are you afraid of?" Seva translated for me.

It was a strange question, I thought, but the Dungan did not get a chance to reply, because at that moment the megaphone squawked above the crowd.

"We've been tricked!" a slanty-eyed guy yelled in Russian, and the banner holder waved the same heavy banner. "Do they want a war? They'll get a war! Let's go on television! They let Bakiev go! Death to Bakiev! Tie him to a tree! Throw stones at him!" He made a pause, and in the megaphone you could hear him swallowing spit. "Bakiev!"

"Olsun," the crowd roared.

"Bakiev!"

"Olsun!"

"Death to Bakiev," Ayana said.

"Let him die," Seva

"Where are we going?" I asked.

"To the television station..." Ayana laughed alluringly.

I took her by the arm, and in a minute the crowd had become a column. Shaking, moving, we were already walking with the crowd in its drowning crush.

The crowd had blocked the road. Pointed hats shone white everywhere. On the sides of the roads, the city dwellers were crowded together. But some of them ran out and joined the column. Cars stayed behind at a respectful distance.

"We're with the people!" White letters on a shop window. A stone went flying. Another stone. The glass fell out with a crash. Part of the crowd ran to the shop, thirty people or so.

"They'll loot it," said Ayana, her hand was moist.

I squeezed more tightly.

We started running.

"You'll all be killed. You'll be beaten up, all of you," a monotonous voice called from the right.

A woman with an exhausted appearance was marching swiftly and broadly. Her dreary speech combined strangely with her swift walk.

"Why are you here, a Russian? There aren't any of your lot here... See, there aren't. They've all gone into hiding... They're scared. Are you brave or something?"

"Don't frighten him," Ayana interrupted jealously.

The woman stared at me, keeping her head straight:

"They're shooting everyone... We'll go to the television station, we'll break the mirror, and they'll shoot... Bullets in the head... I'm twenty-five, I have three children, I work at the market, I don't have any money.. I locked my children in their home, and I came here... I'll be killed, and others will walk over the corpses... Now you'll be killed, and I'll be killed... We'll break the mirror, and we'll all be shot... But I want... I want a bullet in my head..."

We ran around the corner, and when they saw us, people came running after us.

"Oh! The Russians have run away!" the woman livened up.

Five minutes later, the crowd, which had grown while it moved, filled the square in front of the TV center. There weren't any police officers or security guards to be seen. The crowd pushed against the glass doors, which were in fact mirror glass, and it seemed that another crowd was coming towards them. The cry for Bakiev's death hung in the midday air and was reflected: the glass shock and rang out.

"He should be burned!"

I turned around at the cry. I saw many faces that were distorted with rage... Seva's face was calm, he held the camera above his head, pointing it at the sunny sky.

Five minutes after that, a young Kyrgyz man in a grey suit and crooked pink tie came out. He was pale and spoke with barely noticeable irony. He asked: "Who's in charge?"

"He doesn't look in our eyes," the loud woman said. "They should be gouged out."

"How do you say 'eyes'?" I asked.

"Koyozdry," Ayana said.

Ten minutes passed, and they brought a camera out. The crowd moved back, roaring. Orators were found: the one with the banner and the one with the megaphone. Room was made for them, and the guys made speeches in turn, expansive and interrupted, embarrassed and angry, to a yellow microphone that was held out to them. Cut.

"When will it be shown?" the guy with the flag asked piercingly.

"On the evening news."

"You're lying!" The loud woman said furiously and went to the microphone. "Let me say something. Everyone will be killed soon. Shot in the head. At night three women were shot at the bus station. Night will come, it will be cold at night, bullets will fly…"

A revolutionary weather forecast.

"Yok," Ayana shook her head in denial, like a grown-up child who no longer believed in witches.

"Yok," means "No" in Kyrgyz.

There was a shot. Then another. Over our heads. The crowd got anxious, frantic, and people started running away. The last thing that I saw was the TV guy with a pink tie falling down. He clutched his head and fell on his side. Out of fear? Or had he been hit by a bullet? I ran too, caught up in the general flight.

On the northern outskirts, I met Ayana and Seva again. The shooting had stopped.

"Who fired the shots?" I asked.

"Whoever wanted to!" Ayana said cheerfully.

"I have to develop the film," said Seva. "I think I photographed the sniper."

"You won't get an identikit picture," I replied. "You'll just get a mood scene. A landscape and something else."

At the intersection, a girl in a snow-white blouse was directing traffic. She had replaced the overthrown traffic police. She was enjoying the beauty of her gestures. She shone like ice cream. Her swarthy face above the white fabric looked like chocolate.

"Do you like her?" Ayana clipped me around the ear playfully.

We went to walk around the parliament. Ayana took Seva and me in, saying magic words to the security guard, a kid in camouflage clothes. There were a horde of similar kids in camouflage inside the parliament. They had replaced the deputies. The camouflaged youths were sitting in offices. You could hear the banging of hammers, and doors being repaired that had fallen off their hinges. In the corridors, rolled up carpets stood vertically.

"Where's the assembly hall?"

They led us there. The hall was turned upside down, and above the presidium a television was hanging by a thread.

"I took the government building," a gap-toothed guy spoke into my ear and smiled cunningly, showing a silver tooth. "Would you like me to show you? Just don't tell anyone". He took me away to the side. Looking around with a thievish expression, as if afraid of being caught, he began to scroll through photos in his cell phone.

"Bakiev's guards. I saw how much they liked us!" he pointed triumphantly.

"What's with them?" I looked at the figures on the display.

"They turned out not to be real men," he said mysteriously and took the picture away.

The leader of the revolution, Roza, was at the defense ministry. On the way to Roza, we saw institutions that had been set on fire: the prosecutor's office, the tax department. In the latter building, there was still smoke pouring out from the inside, and a fire was smoldering.

We walked up to the iron grill door with a soldier standing by it. By the grill, there were several more people waiting: a man in dark glasses, a rotund old woman, and an old man with deep wrinkles.

"We're here to see Roza," I said.

A frantic administrator came out and asked who we were.

"Journalists."

He disappeared.

"Are you also here to see Roza?" I asked the old man.

"Why would I want to talk to some woman!" He frowned and stomped his foot. "I'm here to see the land minister. I need land…"

Behind the grill, a lanky, pleasant-looking man appeared, with a dazzling smile that did not leave his elongated face.

"Hey! You're Shargunov, aren't you?"

The grill squeaked, and we went into the courtyard.

"I'm Edil. The head of administration in the new government. I returned from emigration today."

He took us up to the second floor. We sat in the foyer by the door to Roza's office. On the wall, portraits of former war ministers hung, the last of them was an empty frame – this morning the former occupier of the emptiness had been arrested.

At last I was taken in to Roza. She had an open face, and was wearing a red jacket, and had glasses on. She was easy to talk to, but this was a somnambulant ease, a soporific charm. I chewed raisins, and Roza bent over her cup.

"I don't have time to sleep. They made me strong tea. So I wouldn't sleep. But if I start talking nonsense or fall asleep, don't be upset…" The door squeaked and someone poked their nose through the gap. Roza raised her voice. "Hey! Are you going to bring the guest tea or not? Is there a draught?" she asked. "Can you feel a draught?"

"Did you expect the revolution?"

"I didn't think it would all happen like this. The revolution came along itself, like wind, it blew some away, and lifted us up… There's a draught, isn't there?"

Roza got up from the table, went to the window, shut it and returned smoothly to her place.

"The ones at the top couldn't, and the ones at the bottom didn't want to, as Lenin said. We were ruled by the bourgeois. If we deceive the people, they will make us answer for it. I meet with people all the time. I go out to them."

"Bakiev olsun?"

I hadn't been brought my tea yet.

"Bakiev olsun," Roza took a sip. "That's what the people demand. But I let him leave the country to stop the slaughter."

"I heard about massacres."

She said something in reply.

"Anteater?" I said, not understanding.

"Banditter."

"How long can you go without sleep? Two days? Three? Where do you get your energy from?"

"I'm a yogi."

My tea was brought to me. I drank a little of it and got up. Seva and Ayana came into the office of the leader of Kyrgyzstan for a minute. My friend took photographs.

"What a strange camera!" Roza said in alarm. "It's not a bomb, is it?"

"Comrade Roza, kill Bakiev!" Ayana made use of the audience.

We went to have lunch.

"I can't see any women in headscarves here, although you're Muslims," Seva said thoughtfully over lunch. "In the neighboring republics there are headscarves, in the Caucasus there are headscarves, even in Kazan everything's different. Women are very free here."

I ate shurpa, he ate manty, and Ayana ordered ice cream and Turkish coffee.

"We're not like the others," she took a drag on her cigarette.

"Kyrgyz women are special. They don't take it in the mouth, but kiss the body," Seva suddenly said.

"Oh, how do you know that?" Ayana took his words to be fitting. She giggled quietly, and covered her face with her wavy hair.

"I lived in Kyrgyzstan. You're wonderful."

"What's the word for 'love'?" I asked.

"Makhabat," they sighed at the same time.

"A furry word," I said. "Sweet, as if a bumblebee had sunk into a flower in the hot sun…"

Ayana looked at me through her hair, which poured over her face. Her eyes burnt with a dazzling fire.

We went out on to the street. By the wall, a large old woman sat, looking as if she was made of cast-iron, with a hand like a scoop, and her motionless arm extended.

"Are you Russian?" I bent down.

She hissed:

"Yes, dear. I'm eighty, and have nothing to eat. I want to kill myself."

I gave her some money.

She crumpled it up, hid it and suddenly gave a lively wink:

"Russians don't give up."

"Do you want to see our taloonchu?" Ayana asked with a laugh.

We wanted to see the bandits.

The taxi driver drove us out of the city. The taxi (like everything else) was incredibly cheap compared to Moscow. And even compared to Chechnya.

Outside the city limits, bandits had gathered in the fields. Taloonchu. That night, they had taken away others' land. There wasn't enough land in these mountainous areas. For many, the overthrow of the regime was an opportunity to seize valuable crumbling pieces of ground.

We drove along a narrow country road. To the left and right, the taloonchu, dressed in dark clothes, were wandering and sitting in the fields. Plastic flasks were sticking out of the loose, rich soil – the captured territory had already been divided up into squares.

"Let me try," I asked Seva.

I got out of the car, held the heavy camera and clicked.

They noticed me. With a dozen cries, a gang ran towards me. They were waving iron bars. For some reason I didn't feel any fear. There was something festive about their cries and running. Happy faces came towards me, their teeth shining, and the heat of jubilation could be felt.

I got into the car, and we drove off. Bang! – a stone hit the bumper. The driver swore. Ayana still found everything terribly funny.

Tomorrow they would start to slaughter and shoot. They would enter the city and kill everyone they saw.

Tomorrow was coming, when the world would learn the news about the massacres here and the latest deaths. Twilight was falling. We wandered around Bishkek, and slogans painted on the walls blended in with the darkness.

"Bakiev – kot". ("Kot means bum," Ayana tactfully translated).

"Invalids against looters". How about that!

There were shots. Bang, bang! Where? Bang! A block away from us? We continued our walk.

We went into a club with neon lights flashing. Ayana had arranged to meet a friend here, also from Osh, who had arrived in Bishkek today. She was called Malika. She was bigger than Ayana, with larger breasts, in a yellow dress, and with theatrically painted lips.

"They paint their lips in the south, and in the north they paint their eyes," Malika explained, drinking white wine.

On a stool by the bar, a huge Kyrgyz man in a blue tracksuit was perched, getting drunk, and waving his arms:

"So we went into Adidas, you see. The saleswoman said don't break anything. Take any clothes you want. We left our old clothes there. We put them in a heap."

The barman listened enviously.

"Let's go to the mountains," Malika suggested.

In a corner above the bar the revolutionary television was playing. There were photographs displayed on the screen.

"Bakiev killed them. The bastard," Malika said with conviction. "Damn, it's boring, there aren't many people around, everyone wants to set something on fire. It's fun in the mountains." She elbowed Ayana: "Tell them!"

We went out and ran into a street procession. There were young people, and in front of them was a leader with a stick. There was strong-willed anger in his movements. The neon sign lit up his glassy stare. And then I realized: it wasn't a stick, but a long Winchester rifle. He went into the club, and the whole crowd followed him.

"What a bunch of zombies," Malika said disapprovingly.

The girls spluttered with laughter.

Behind the buildings, very close by, there was a shot. Bang! Silence. Then another shot.

The taxi drove us through the center, past the white house. There were candles by the fence. There were a lot of people squatting around the tent.

At night we went into the mountains. Here there was a lively health resort which had frozen in 1985. There were clichéd announcements. "Comrade holiday-makers!" "Kyrgyz SSR". We went to the swimming pool, where there was murky light, thick steam, and hot spring water. On the tiled walls were peeling, swollen, rotten pictures of Soviet health.

There was no one there but us. The swimming pool was large, and we swam in pairs to different ends. Ayana dipped her head in. It was a charming sight: her closed, narrow eyes. Her slanty eyelids….

I stroked her wet head. The water swayed us to and fro, stronger and stronger, and became boiling.

"Let's go to Naryn tomorrow," she murmured.

"Huh? OK, let's."

"Do you want to go to Osh?"

"Osh? I'd go anywhere with you…"

Then we stood outside, Bishkek was somewhere below us, and the dark mountains were all around us. The stars were close, many of them. Ayana pressed herself to me and gently kissed my neck, and higher up my face to my temple, as if repeating a pattern of the stars with her lips.

I felt completely alone, and as if I could read the future now.

In an hour, for example, I would be a hair's breadth from death, but would survive, but one time I would not survive.

I read the future without regret or interest, as if everything that could happen had already taken place.

As if I were not an insignificant mortal, but a green star above the mountains.

A BOOK WITHOUT PHOTOGRAPHS

The car honked, and started moving.
We got in the taxi and drove away from the mountains.
Towards the dawn and the riots.

# Voskresenki

What does it mean if the camera tells you: "Memory card error"?

Obviously I'm still young. Yes or no? You must agree with me: I'm still young.

And still, looking back, going over the pictures from my life, I already think: there was an error somewhere. I want to find out the plan, the task of my life.

Where was the error? Or was everything honest and correct, and the pictures will come together over time? It was rough, it was heady, but it was the way it was supposed to be. The childish contrast of long ago – a priest among pioneers – was right. And my sudden longing for Soviet times during the sudden drunken time was right as well. And it was right to go into literature, to "Novy Mir" with short stories, and not into TV journalism. And it was right to marry the uncooperative and wild Anya – because it was following the dictates of passion, and because the bright girl had given me a bright-eyed son. And going into politics, into the snow storm, on to the street, under flags, to the angry and abandoned peers was also the right move. The defeat was regrettable, but was still valuable, it still gave me joy in my heart that I did not break, I did not break, no, I didn't break. And the war trips…. And solitude. And this album of mine with invisible photographs was important to someone invisible.

I live near the Molodyozhnaya Metro Station – I rent a one-room apartment in a long building block surrounded by ten buildings that look identical. My job is to write. I write for many different publications. On weekends I collect my son, and we go for a walk. He stays with me on Saturday night. We go to the park, to the circus, and sometimes to church.

Vanya is more interested in going to church than I was at his age. There he is meek and enchanted.

Life experience has not hardened me. But I have become distrustful. I don't trust people very much. I only trust the most generous of them – readers. My new comrades are readers. The ones who need the words I write. Although readers also sometimes grow cool.

"Who is the person closest to me?" repeating this question from the Gospels, I reply to myself "The most distant". The more distant the person is, the closer they are. I want to trust the first people I meet, who don't need anything from me at all. It seems to me that a simple and random person can reveal something very important. It constantly seems that the wind will blow, it will turn a page, and the new page will dazzle with the brightness of the photos. This is probably the remains of youth talking within me.

But for some reason, I know for certain, I don't even doubt it, that a passionate love awaits me in the future.

To end, I would like to tell you about the last farmer. I met him thanks to Dimon.

Dimon is my age, he's one of my readers from Dzerzhinsk, he drinks heavily and does his work. He's a gangster or a businessman, or rather both one and the other.

He read one of my books, then another one, and wrote me a letter. We drank together when he came to Moscow, and the next day he persuaded me to come with him to show me a village that was dear to his heart.

It was a hot summer, and together with this summer the village of Voskresenki stood in one of the central regions of Russia. Dimon often made trips there in his jeep. He visited a house where his grandmother once lived. By the end of the day she fell into a blissful state, and sitting by the dreary window, outside of which there was a crooked path down to the river, the water shimmered, and the forest on the other shore grew dark, she would ask quietly: "What station is this?", and then, a little slower, with dignity: "Which is the next one?"

I stood on the porch, thinking: so you're in the countryside, but your father is also from the countryside, and your grandmother, and grandfather, great-grandfather, great-grandmother, and great-great.... Is your native Vyatka village intact? Or has the taiga closed in over it? You should look for an answer in the countryside. Here you'll realize how to live further. Well? What do you feel?

I didn't feel anything apart from the bites of nasty gadflies.

The village was almost empty, there were only a few old women left. I read about one of them on a post next to the shop, and remembered it word for word: "Zoya Porfirevena Yegorova, eighty-eight years old, left her home and did not return". Her home – that meant a crooked hut. She did not return – that meant that she got dizzy or twisted her ankle, and fell down somewhere and disappeared: in a pit or in the forest.

In summer there were more people – dacha owners, Dimon explained. But the link with the outside world was complicated: only by car.

Early the next morning, after stocking up at the shop with vodka, canned food, two cans of beer and one ice cream, we drove to the cemetery.

At the village cemetery I met the last farmer.

First we saw a tractor that was crawling along the outskirts of the cemetery and dragging a load of logs on a trailer.

We were sitting on a rotting bench by the first grave, the bees were buzzing and the butterflies were flitting about, from the stone a fairy-tale grandfather and grandmother were looking at us out of oval eggs with golden rims, who were only lacking a speckled hen.

Dimon jumped up.

"Volodya! Vovchik! Buddy!" he waved his arms towards the windscreen of the tractor that was blinding from the sun.

The tractor stopped, still shuddering and emitting smoke, and a man with a wrinkled, happy face jumped out.

"Hello, uncle Volodya," Dima said more respectfully, when the man came up to us. "Can I pour you something?"

The man firmly shook out hands – his palm with rough with blisters.

"I don't drink until twelve," he gave his sparkling blue eye a cunning wink. "Like that... Bismark..." he smoked and shook in a coughing laugh, and became just like the tractor, which was shuddering and smoking in the distance. "And I'm at work. I'm hauling things for the big shots."

"What big shots?" I asked.

"City folk, they're building a dacha."

"Then visit us in the afternoon," Dima said. "We'll treat you. Why don't you show Seryozha the cemetery?"

"Sure, that won't take long..." The man put his arm around my shoulder, leaned his head over to mine, and whispered: "All my children are here... I can give you a tour. I often come here. I can name them all with my eyes closed..."

We went into the bushes of the cemetery, the firm gravestones were replaced with old, crumbling ones, and the further we went, the more overgrown it was, the more wretchedly the weeds towered, and the insects swarmed louder and abundantly.

We walked, and my guide leafed through an album of dead people before me.

"That one was a tractor driver like me. A tree fell on him and crushed him" – he pointed to a stern, puckered face. "And that's my uncle Grisha, who drowned. My father, who suffered from his injuries, he fought in the war, and my mother was a worker, God rest her soul. This is Granny Frosya, she was kind, she put up with all of us, and my grandfather Ignaty Kuzmich, a real character... Quite a clown! He could sew, he stole a flag on the May holidays and made himself underpants out of it... When he got drunk, he'd run out on to the road just in his red underwear and dance..."

He grabbed me by the shoulder again, with frightening animal strength, and his long nails pierced my shirt... "There, look..." In a clumsy dance, we staggered to the most distant edge of the cemetery. "There they are, my sons, have a look!" Among the grass, there were two mounds that looked strange and wild, all covered in grass, but small and mown. He let go of me, swayed and rubbed his eye with his fist.

"Vasya and Lyosha. Vasya was twelve, he had an infection... Lyoshka was three, he had a lung inflammation..."

"What about doctors?"

"The ambulance didn't come. They said it was too far."

"How about putting crosses on the graves?"

"What crosses..."

"Where are the photographs then?"

"I don't have any photographs of them. I don't even have one of myself. So it's early for us to die yet. Send a photographer – let him go nuts. Then I can go into the ground. Is that right? Who needs those photos of yours? Flowers grow in the field, I walk and remember my sons. The grass grows, as if it were their hair. Once a week I mow here, so it doesn't get overgrown. When our time comes, we'll do everything properly."

"And where's their mother?"

"She hanged herself. She was a drunk. She left, abandoning me with the children, went to live with a fellow drunk and hanged herself at the regional center. My brother also hanged himself. So did my eldest son. But he's not here, he's near Ryazan."

"So you're alone?"

"Aha. Are you married?"

"Separated."

"Why's that?"

"Um..."

"Do you have children?"
"A son."
"You need to look after him."
"Do you have a lot of work to do, Volodya?"
"I heat the bathhouse on Sundays. I dig up the garden with the tractor," he mumbled in embarrassment. "I was a submariner, in the military. I travelled halfway around the world in the submarine. But that was way back... Then I gathered peat on the farm here. There were a lot of us, healthy and hard-working. And the old people were employed: we used to have cows and sheep. There was a school, club and sanatorium. And there was a light railway through the forest. A lot of us country people working in town – you get on the train at night, the car rattles off and in the morning you're there. Later, when all this nonsense started, the trains stopped running. We even went out to protest, asking to get our train back, we made some noise, and then we saw that the railway was in disrepair, we had stolen pieces of it ourselves. Now when you go into the forest, there's something shining. Like snakes. Some pieces of metal were left behind, not many, but they are there."

"But generally, how do you live?" I suddenly asked with an unaccountable hope.

"In summer I'm fine – there are lots of people from the town, and I can get some extra cash. Things are terrible in winter. In winter the wolves howl. There's more of them every year, on the New Year one of them came by... It ran into the garden, it really had some nerve. I shot it, I have a double-barreled shotgun, otherwise it would have killed our grannies..." Uncle Volodya beamed from his joke, his wrinkles smoothed for a while, and he smoked again. "On dacha owner has a good boy. He looks like my Vasechka and he's also called Vasya. He's scared of thunder, but I'm trying to teach him not to be. Bang bang, I say, it's me, uncle thunder! His mother lies out in the sun, and we play together... All right, let's go. I need to do some more ploughing."

The man went a step ahead of me from the weeds to the exit, to the iron gates of the cemetery, which had once been blue and were now reddish, with a five-cornered rusty star. He was hunched over, and limped a little. He turned around.

"Are you here for long," he asked, squinting with an inquiring blue spark in his eyes.

"No."

"Ah… I need an assistant. To raise some animals. I'd drive the tractor, and you'd look after the goats. Women don't come here. There was a cow, but I had it put down. If someone could have helped me with it, I might have got some rest…. But there was nothing but disappointment… But there's nowhere else to go. It's like a submarine! Nicht kapitulieren! Power and strength! Am I right? I tell Dimka: move here, bring your family, and we'll live like human beings…"

"How should we live?" I asked. "How? Seriously…"

Volodya opened his mouth in a smile in which half the teeth were missing:

"Build up your muscle! Do push-ups. Go for runs. Do sit-ups. I get exercise doing chores – I dig and mow, and my heart is glad!"

"And that's it?"

"That's to start with!"

The last peasant of the village of Voskresenki turned around and walked toward the cemetery exit.

Dear Reader,

Thank you for purchasing this book.

We at Glagoslav Publications are glad to welcome you, and hope that you find our books to be a source of knowledge and inspiration.

We want to show the beauty and depth of the Slavic region to everyone looking to expand their horizon and learn something new about different cultures, different people, and we believe that with this book we have managed to do just that.

Now that you've got to know us, we want to get to know you. We value communication with our readers and want to hear from you! We offer several options:

- ❖ Join our Book Club on Goodreads, Library Thing and Shelfari, and receive special offers and information about our giveaways;
- ❖ Share your opinion about our books on Amazon, Barnes & Noble, Waterstones and other bookstores;
- ❖ Join us on Facebook and Twitter for updates on our publications and news about our authors;
- ❖ Visit our site www.glagoslav.com to check out our Catalogue and subscribe to our Newsletter.

Glagoslav Publications is getting ready to release a new collection and planning some interesting surprises — stay with us to find out!

Glagoslav Publications

Office 36, 88-90 Hatton Garden

EC1N 8PN London, UK

Tel: + 44 (0) 20 32 86 99 82

Email: contact@glagoslav.com

Glagoslav Publications Catalogue

- *The Time of Women* by Elena Chizhova
- *Sin* by Zakhar Prilepin
- *Hardly Ever Otherwise* by Maria Matios
- *The Lost Button* by Irene Rozdobudko
- *Khatyn* by Ales Adamovich
- *Christened with Crosses* by Eduard Kochergin
- *The Vital Needs of the Dead* by Igor Sakhnovsky
- *METRO 2033* (Dutch Edition) by Dmitry Glukhovsky
- *A Poet and Bin Laden* by Hamid Ismailov
- *White Shanghai* by Elvira Baryakina
- *The Stone Bridge* by Alexander Terekhov
- *King Stakh's Wild Hunt* by Uladzimir Karatkevich
- *Andrei Tarkovsky: the Collector of Dreams* by Layla Alexander-Garrett
- *Depeche Mode* by Serhii Zhadan
- *Moryak* by Lee Mandel
- *Harlequin's Costume* by Leonid Yuzefovich
- *A Book Without Photographs* by Sergei Shargunov
- *The Sarabande of Sara's Band* by Larysa Denysenko
- *Herstories, An Anthology of New Ukrainian Women Prose Writers*
- *Watching The Russians* (Dutch Edition) by Maria Konyukova
- *The Hawks of Peace* by Dmitry Rogozin
- *The Grand Slam and Other Stories* (Dutch Edition) by Leonid Andreev

More coming soon...

www.ingramcontent.com/pod-product-compliance
Lightning Source LLC
Chambersburg PA
CBHW020907080526
44589CB00011B/481